D0592290

RABELAIS AND PANURGE

a psychological approach
to literary character

by

MARY E. RAGLAND

© Editions Rodopi N.V., Amsterdam 1976
Printed in the Netherlands
ISBN: 90–6203–339–3

For Henry

TABLE OF CONTENTS

INTRODUCTION

Rabelais's Panurge has long charmed and puzzled critics who tend to agree that although problematic, he is the soul of Rabelais's work. Appearing in all the books except *Gargantua,* Panurge manifests surprisingly different character traits from book to book and thereby elicits questions not only about his unity and evolution, but ultimately about his function and importance in the whole of Rabelais's work.[1] Traditionally, critical studies have emphasized Panurge's stylistic function, viewing him as pretext for satire and comedy. Recently, some studies have portrayed Panurge as a purely linguistic entity, present in the work as one more example of Rabelais's fundamental ambiguity, whether as representative of a linguistic system of binary oppositions or as reflection of Rabelais's arbitrary alternation between *écriture* and *parole.*[2]

In addition to Panurge's essential stylistic and linguistic functions, there still remains for analysis the sensory impression left by this fictional character. In this study, then, I shall talk about Panurge as a real and believable character who attains an emotional reality because of his impact on the reader. Such a perspective does not conflict with stylistic and linguistic interpretations; rather, it makes a connection between processes of the human psyche and the text.[3] Seen from a twentieth century psychological perspective, one can view the act of reading as a mimetic process: "truth" is in the reader who "re-creates" textual meaning through emotional as well as intellectual tensions. By focusing on an emotional rhythm, seen as the cohesive element in Rabelais's

1. I shall follow standard critical procedure and not discuss the Panurge of *Le Cinquième Livre* because of the controversy surrounding the authenticity of its authorship.

2. This general reference is to Jean Paris, *Hamlet et Panurge* (Paris: Editions du Seuil, 1971) and Floyd Gray, *Rabelais et l'Ecriture* (Paris: Librairie A.-G. Nizet, 1974).

3. E. Benveniste has pointed out: ". . . la différence profonde entre le langage comme système de signes et le langage assumé comme exercice par l'individu" E. Benveniste, *Problèmes de linguistique générale* (Paris: Gallimard, 1966), p. 254.

books and which is said to be microcosmically portrayed by Panurge, one can then view Rabelais's paradoxical and ambiguous work in terms of the dynamics of human feelings (tensions) and fantasies (central themes). Insofar as his work is apparently loosely-knit in construction and since much of his material is primal and elemental (farcical humor, scatalogical references, fairy tales and so forth), one can readily discuss Rabelais in terms of the basic dynamics of feeling and fantasy.

Multifaceted Panurge is alternately a rogue, a rebel, a joyful fellow, a farcical stock type character, a doubtful and frightened person and a total coward. A character configuration which includes, in varying degrees, all these countenances is that of a child seeking to create an identity in and rapport with his society. In his desire for attention a child is often roguish, rebellious or comic; frustrated by a world which he does not understand or cannot explain, the child is frequently frightened and insecure. In his reactions to the world around him, the child could be considered a symbol of uncivilized, "natural" man; insofar as his responses are largely governed by the spontaneity of immediate and direct emotional reaction, he could be viewed as a "pure" type of emotional man.

Panurge is portrayed in this study as a character who is unified from book to book by a pattern of child-like behavior. Natural, spontaneous, asocial, rebellious, comic and fearful, Panurge interacts with wise Pantagruel to bring the central themes of Rabelais's work to life. In *Pantagruel* Panurge, adored by his friends, manifests a limitless egotism. In *Le Tiers Livre* Pantagruel assumes the role of father figure; he pays Panurge's debts and insists that he act in a more socially acceptable manner. Although Panurge acquiesces, he is frustrated by the sudden loss of security and identity. His symbolic attempt to adapt to societal demands takes the form of a quest for a suitable wife. However, no one can provide him with a blueprint for the correct choice. Unable to accept either the emotional insecurities occasioned by his doubts or the restraints of adult responsibility, he decides to continue his quest in unknown lands. In *Le Quart Livre* he loses even the emotional support of familiarity and is thus reduced to a state of cowardice and infantile fear.

Twentieth century findings from psychology provide critical support for the interpretation of Panurge as child-like man as well as for the idea that readers respond to certain literary characters through the emotions as well as through the intellect. Thus, readers are said to be drawn to Panurge, in part through the emotional residue of feelings and fantasies from their own experiences in childhood as well as in context of the basic physiological structure of the emotional dynamics which enable one to "re-create" character. Linking language and meaning, author's vision and reader's response, literary character is said to be "real" insofar as it embodies the emotional dynamics of a work. This study views Panurge's quest for certainty and identity as an emotional correlative of the intellectual quest which is implicitly marked by questioning and doubting and has thus encouraged many critics to view Panurge as a symbol of the philosophical concept of relativity. That he does not in fact arrive at emotional maturity or philosophical certainty is unimportant if one considers his significance in the whole of Rabelais's work. Joyous and rebellious, certain and doubting, serious and comic, seeking and resisting, Panurge embodies the essence of the work.

Finally, if one considers that the farcical character, the rogue, the buffoon and the clown, all well-known literary types, do behave in ways which strongly resemble what I have labeled, from a psychological viewpoint, child-like behavior, then perhaps it may not seem difficult to "suspend disbelief" and view a thirty-five year old man and a cardboard pastiche of a real person as symbol of what is universally and eternally child-like in man, that element which is free from inscription in rational and logical systematization and socialization – the soul of Rabelais's work.[4]

---

4. My view of literary interpretation fundamentally agrees with Norman Holland who has sought to demonstrate in "Unity Identity Text Self," pp. 813-22 in *PMLA*, 90, 1975, that: "all of us, as we read, use the literary work to symbolize and finally to replicate ourselves" (p. 816). In other words, critics and readers perceive and experience their texts in terms of their own identities. Holland gives the equation: unity is to text as identity is to self. Unity and identity are seen as invariables and text and self are seen as variables. Thus, every critic like every text includes both continuity and change, a constant theme against which a sequence of variations is played. (pp. 815-16). In my interpretation of the child-like aspects of Panurge, those aspects would correspond to Holland's concept of a variable in the text which finds a correlative variable in my "self" and may be accessible to any other reader as well.

CHAPTER I: METHOD IN PERSPECTIVE–
PANURGE AND HIS CRITICS

Despite the scholarly interest in Panurge, most studies of this multiform character are brief or merely include him in a general study of various aspects of Rabelais's work. Since I am offering a full-length study of the character himself, it will be helpful to pinpoint some of the specific problems he raises. That Panurge is critically problematic is made clearly obvious by the amount of disagreement and contradiction among critics on fundamental issues. Most discussions center around two issues: Who is Panurge and thus what is his significance in Rabelais's work? Is there unity or evolution of character from book to book?

In answer to 'Who is Panurge? ' many critics point out that he is a recognizable stock type character, present in the work mostly for comic purposes. His source is thought to be possibly the *Macaronaci Opus,* burlesque poems written in Macaronic Latin by Teofilo Folengo, a monk of the twelfth century. The twelfth of these poems introduces Cingar a seeming prototype of Panurge.[1] Or, tracing Panurge's source to medieval fabliaux characters, Besant and Tetel emphasize that like these types he is crafty, deceptive and marked by a cruel humor.[2] Fleury cites the motive of poverty for Panurge's deceptiveness and cruelty, placing him in the lineage of Villon and thus giving him some depth of character.[3]

Going beyond a concrete view of Panurge as rogue and farcical type, many critics stress his symbolic role as a spokesman for Rabelais's personal and intellectual battles. In Rocques' opinion Rabelais has given

---

1. L'Association des Amis de Rabelais et de la Devinière, *Les Amis de Rabelais et de la Devinière,* Bulletin No. 3, II (1964), 95, and also William Frances Smith, *Rabelais in His Writings* (New York: G. P. Putnam's Sons, 1918), pp. 28-31.

2. Marcel Tetel, *Rabelais* (New York: Twayne Publications, Inc., 1967), pp. 26-27, and Walter Besant, *Rabelais* (London: William Blackwood and Sons, 1879), p. 98.

3. Jean Fleury, *Rabelais et ses Oeuvres* (Paris: Didier et Cie, Librairies-Editeurs, 1877), p. 358.

Panurge the task of illustrating the contradictory views associated with the "Querelle des Femmes" and the subject of marriage.[4] Tetel and Screech observe that Panurge is a mouthpiece for the philosophical and theological battles which Rabelais waged against the Sorbonne and the Catholic Church.[5]

Many critics view Panurge as Rabelais's *moi intime,* a direct expression of Rabelais's personal frustrations. For Tetel and Glauser Panurge represents the kind of carefree life Rabelais would have enjoyed, but never fully experienced. And perhaps, say these critics, Panurge's quest for a wife is the literary substitute for the marriage Rabelais never had.[6] Whatever critics may think about 'who Panurge is' in terms of source or import for Rabelais the man, most agree that his importance in the whole of the work is to symbolize Rabelais's philosophy of the human condition.

Panurge enters Rabelais's work in the first book written (*Pantagruel,* chapter ix). Pantagruel sees Panurge from a distance and as though magnetically drawn to him, he approaches and asks these questions which can be interpreted as basic philosophic questions regarding the nature of man: "Qui estes vous? Dont venez vous? Où allez vous? Que querez vous? Et quel est vostre nom? "[7] *Pantagruel, Le Tiers Livre* and *Le Quart Livre* provide answers to these questions. In *Pantagruel* Panurge gives concrete answers, explaining that he was born and reared as a child in Touraine. Marvelous adventures have marked his life, the most recent being his escape from Turkey where he had been taken prisoner. The reader gradually comes to envision Panurge as a strong-willed character, with definite opinions about everything. In *Pantagruel,* he is an amusing fellow, a trickster, a braggart, a fun-lover and sometimes a coward. In *Le Tiers Livre* and *Le Quart Livre* the symbolic import of Panurge often obscures his concrete aspects. In *Le Tiers Livre* Panurge asks all the representatives of all the doctrines and institutions in the

---

4. Mario Rocques, "Aspects de Panurge," in *Ouvrage publié pour le Quatrième Centenaire de sa Mort, 1553-1953* (Genève: Librairie E. Droz, 1953), p. 129.
   5. Tetel, p. 28, and M. A. Screech, *The Rabelaisian Marriage: Aspects of Rabelais's Religion, Ethics and Comic Philosophy* (London: Edward Arnold Ltd., 1958), p. 60.
   6. Tetel, p. 28 and Alfred Glauser, *Rabelais créateur* (Paris: Editions A.-G. Nizet, 1966), p. 52 and pp. 130 and 132.
   7. Rabelais, *Pantagruel, Oeuvres Complètes,* vol. I, ed., Pierre Jourda (Paris: Editions Garnier Frères, 1962), p. 264.

France of his time, all the known and respected authorities, in other words, if he should marry and if he does so, will he be cuckolded. In *Le Quart Livre* Panurge continues his quest into foreign territory where he meets with hostile and deceptive powers, still finding no answers to his questions. Thus, many critics emphasize that Panurge's quest in *Le Tiers Livre* and *Le Quart Livre* illustrates a moral and philosophical lesson which teaches that there is no absolute truth. Panurge is said, thus, to function as a catalyst to Rabelais's creative doubt.

Interpretations of Panurge's specific philosophical significance vary greatly despite the general agreement that he symbolizes Rabelais's philosophical vision. Muir emphasizes that he is a symbol of the double aspect of human nature, a man of sound natural appetites and of great intelligence because he considers questions from all points of view.[8] Tetel stresses that Panurge is a symbol of individual freedom, possibly even a *révolté* who seeks personal liberty in speech and action beyond anything else.[9] Screech, on the contrary, views Panurge as the symbolic antithesis of the liberty presumably admired by Rabelais, an indecisive, sinful character who teaches a positive moral lesson by showing one how not to be.[10] And taking a middle position, Glauser portrays a Panurge who represents the Rabelaisian belief in the necessity of avoiding extremes.[11]

Related to the critical opinions about Panurge's source and significance in Rabelais's work is the question of whether or not he is a unified character. Although recent studies, informed by linguistic theories, even question whether he is a character at all, most critics of Rabelais have viewed Panurge as a character, be he comic stock type or symbolic *porte-parole*. However, there is much disagreement on the issues of unity and evolution of character.[12] Critics who have commented on this problem generally find a basic unity *in* the character of

8. Edwin Muir, *Essays on Literature and Society* (Cambridge: Harvard University Press, 1965), pp. 179-80.

9. Tetel, p. 28.

10. Screech, pp. 64-65.

11. Glauser, p. 49.

12. Mario Rocques states the problem well: "Panurge sans unité, dit l'un, constance de caractère, dit l'autre, opposition voulue de l'évangélisme de Pantagruel et de la superstition de Panurge pense celui-ci, mais, pour un autre, contraste esthétique habilement balancé de Panurge le couard et de Frère Jean le brave." Mario Rocques, "Aspects de Panurge," pp. 122-23.

Panurge, the various traits of his personality seen as different aspects of the same traits. Besant points out that the braggart of *Pantagruel* is merely a more egocentric version of the "real" character, the coward of *Le Quart Livre*.[13] Lefranc attributes Panurge's evolution of behavior to the increasing realism of Rabelais's style which progressively removes layers of illusion to reveal Panurge's basic personality as it always has been.[14] He sees very little distance between the egotist of *Pantagruel,* the *beau parleur* of *Le Tiers Livre* and the coward of *Le Quart Livre.* Lebègue views this development of Panurge's behavior as an example of constancy of character, attributable to Rabelais's Renaissance adhesion to the suggestion of the Ancients that characters should be constant in order to be universal.[15]

The question of evolution of character is ultimately inseparable from the problem of unity of character. Among those critics who comment on Panurge's evolution one quickly delineates three distinct positions. Either, Panurge's evolution is attributed to factors extrinsic to the character himself such as Rabelais's stylistic development and philosophical enrichment; or, Panurge's evolution is said to issue from within the character. For example, Rocques depicts a complex Panurge whose growing conflict and indecision is said to lead him from a sense of omnipotence to a position of powerlessness.[16] Finally, Panurge is said by some critics not to evolve at all. His essential function remains stylistic and thus one cannot speak of him as a character because he changes constantly. Glauser calls him "le jeu pur" and Gray says that he is at each moment "passage et métamorphose".[17]

Finally, most critical evaluations of Panurge also consider his changes of behavior in comparison with the changes of the other characters, most agreeing that while the other characters change profoundly and continually, Panurge remains essentially the same. Panurge's changes are said to be superficial, the unveiling of a doubting insecure person who finishes where he begins. Glauser and Gray, on the contra-

---

13. Besant, p. 104.

14. Abel Lefranc, *Rabelais: Etudes sur Gargantua, Pantagruel, Le Tiers Livre* (Paris: A Michel, 1953), pp. 260-61.

15. Raymond Lebègue, *Rabelais* (Tubingen: Max Niemeyer Verlag, 1952), pp. 10-11.

16. Rocques, "Aspects de Panurge," pp. 129-30.

17. Glauser, p. 130 and Floyd Gray, *Rabelais et l'Ecriture* (Paris: Librairie A.-G. Nizet, 1974), p. 114.

ry, feel that a specific and unified character structure would inhibit Panurge's implicit stylistic function of incarnating the liberty and movement which is ultimately that of the text confined within the limitations of words which it, nonetheless, constantly seeks to transcend.[18]

My interpretation of Panurge is not antithetic to the existing body of commentary; rather, my study synthesizes contradictory views in its attempt to explain the acknowledged enigma that is Panurge. The specific focus is a twentieth century interpretation of a sixteenth century character. This study will not try to "re-create" a sixteenth century Panurge, the Panurge supposedly intended by Rabelais, as historical scholars advise, nor will it talk of Panurge as representative of Rabelais's unconscious being. Although it will deal with Panurge as specific character type, as comic character and as representative of Rabelaisian doubt, this study will emphasize the emotional aspect of his various sides and its potential impact on the reader, rather than stylistic or philosophic meaning.

Glauser says that there is no psychological unity in Panurge because he is a "personnage en formation."[19] This statement might be reversed to say that Panurge is a unified character because of the fact that he is a person in formation. Unified by an emotional substructure of child-like behavior, Panurge as "child" in the process of becoming adult is cared for by Pantagruel, who, in the role of guide for and counselor to Panurge, is a kind of father figure. According to the best-known critics, Pantagruel represents intelligence, wisdom, reason, goodness, common sense. Panurge, on the contrary, is unlearned, insensitive, mischievous, irrational. The characteristics attributed to Pantagruel would describe an ideally mature adult; those attributed to Panurge could characterize the egotistical, unsocialized aspects of a child. In *Pantagruel,* Panurge is happy and carefree, protected and adored by those around him. Such is the paradise of childhood where the world is yet to be conquered. In *Le Tiers Livre* the beautiful childhood dream is destroyed when Pantagruel pays Panurge's debts, demanding that his companion henceforth become a responsible adult. In *Le Tiers Livre* and *Le Quart Livre,* Panurge embarks on a quest to find a wife, in other words, a quest to settle down within society; this can be viewed as the emotional quest of the child for maturity.

18. Glauser, pp. 123 and 130, and Gray, p. 114.
19. Glauser, p. 132.

Many critics have spoken of the creative potential for learning and intellectual growth which is implicit in Rabelais's essential doubt. This study will emphasize the importance of a corollary kind of growth. Emotional uncertainty, embodied by Panurge in *Le Tiers Livre* and *Le Quart Livre*, can create conflict which may serve as a catalyst to possible growth. An ability to compromise, a sense of responsibility towards others, an awareness of an inner strength which may help one to face the vicissitudes of life, are some of the qualities of emotional balance which may be learned. One speaks, then, of the integrative quest in Rabelais — a search for emotional strength issuing from and combined with the growth of intellectual awareness. Panurge will be considered as representative of this emotional quest for maturity, and the meaning of his successes and failures will be viewed in the context of Rabelais's total work.

Before describing the specific critical perspective underlying my view of Panurge, it may help to set up a provisional delineation of various critical approaches to literary works and their implied treatment of literary character. One might speak, for instance, of historic, mythic and modern. An historic approach tends to view the characters within their period of creation. Much biographical material and supposition about the author's life, relationships and intellectual stances are used. M. A. Screech is a well-known proponent of such a critical perspective. In an historic context, Panurge is usually seen as a character drawn directly from popular literary sources of the period in which Rabelais composed his work. Whether or not critics who subscribe to an historic perspective feel that Panurge's source is directly traceable, they give the following explanation for his presence in the total work: Panurge is the ideal *porte-parole* for Rabelais's intellectual battles and for his philosophical ideas, ideal because censors of the period will hopefully not admit to any seriousness of commentary expressed by a farcical character. Thus, Panurge's comic nature takes on the hue of a disguise in the service of philosophical/political necessity.

A mythic approach stresses the historical impact of Greek mythology on later literary developments as well as the universal existence of fixed character types. A partisan of this critical perspective is Ludwig Schrader who has drawn a comparison between Panurge and Hermes.[20]

20. Ludwig Schrader, *Panurge und Hermes: Zum Ursprung eines Charakters bei Rabelais* (Bonn: Romanisches Seminar der Universität Bonn, 1958).

Historic and mythic criticisms tend to see literary character from a direct viewpoint while modern criticism leans toward an abstract view of character. The critical perspective which labels itself modern is usually eclectic, making use of philosophy, history, anthropology, biography, psychology, sociology, political science, linguistics and so forth in order to elucidate the text at hand. From a philosophical viewpoint, for example, Panurge may be seen as expressive of existentially "free" man. Or, from a generalized psychological view Panurge has been discussed as Rabelais's *moi intime*. To my knowledge, there are no psychoanalytic studies of Rabelais, either Freudian, drawing a direct connection between the actions of the characters and the conscious and unconscious elements in the author's life history, or Jungian, appealing to a mystical psychology supposed to be at the source of artistic creation.[21] From a Marxist stance, Henri Lefebvre depicts a bourgeois Panurge and Bakhtin does stress the inherent peasant and folk aspect of Rabelais's Renaissance comedy. Stucturalists and semiotic linguists see the literary work as a closed world of multiple signs, the *signifiants*; the various meanings given to these signs by critics are the *signifiés* which are considered to be statements of all the possible questions posed by a work, rather than explicit meanings.[22] Partisan critic Jean Paris thus views Panurge as inseparable from the linguistic milieu in which he exists. Stylistic critics tend to use various sources of "proof" in order to emphasize the essentially technical function of character.

Of course, this brief and simple list of critical methods and their exponents does not pretend to do credit to the richness and diversity of the body of Rabelaisian scholarship and has been included only for the purpose of pointing out that despite the various differences, most of these critics have one important thing in common. They all focus their criticism on the text and/or the author. My study will attempt to depart from this bias by focusing on the third element in the literary process – the reader. Those critics who think that reading should be a purely aesthetic experience believe that the most advanced reader, the critic, can be wholly rational and disinterested in relation to the text

---

21. Frederick C. Crews, "Literature and Psychology," pp. 73-87 in *Relations of Literary Study: Essays on Interdisciplinary Contributions*, ed. James Thorpe (New York: Modern Language Association, 1967), p. 81.

22. Serge Doubrovsky, *Pourquoi la nouvelle critique: Critique et objectivité* (Paris: Mercure de France, 1967), p. 93.

being interpreted.[23] One can certainly agree that as a reader develops into a capable critic, he becomes more detached from an emotional manner of reading. As he considers the multitude of elements that compose a work of literary art, the critic may take into account various operative factors such as genre, style, history, audience and so forth. Adept at deciphering complex meanings of a work, critics becomes guides who lead less advanced readers to a more intellectual appreciation of a work. On the other hand, one may contend that critics, such as José Ortega y Gasset, are incorrect in the view that any emotional response by the reader is an uncritical or inferior reaction. In a paraphrase, Wayne Booth says that Ortega feels that a reader's pleasure should spring from the "aesthetic" and intellectual qualities of the work; the reading experience should be form contemplated rather than form experienced.[24] Booth cites a translation of Ortega's theory:

> Not only is grieving and rejoicing at such human destinies as a work of art presents and narrates a very different thing from true artistic pleasure, but preoccupation with the human content of the work is in principle incompatible with aesthetic enjoyment proper.... Tears and laughter are aesthetically frauds.[25]

This study, on the contrary, theorizes a close relationship between a reader's intellectual recognition of and emotional reaction to character in a literary work. Although intellectual and stylistic components in Rabelais's work will be considered, the major emphasis will be on reader emotional response to character seen as an emotional entity.

Wayne C. Booth in *The Rhetoric of Fiction* sets up four perspectives from which one may regard literature as it affects readers: (1) works viewed as reflections of reality — truth; (2) works viewed as expressions of the author's mind and soul — sincerity; (3) works viewed as realizations of formal excellence — coherence, complexity, unity, harmony; (4) works viewed as they affect readers — interest. Booth expands upon these categories, saying that the critic who emphasizes the first and second perspectives is largely interested in the intellectual or cognitive value of the work: "We have, or can be made to have, strong intellectual curiosity about 'the facts', the true interpretation, the true reasons,

---

23. Frederick C. Crews, "Anaesthetic Criticism: I," pp. 31-35 in *The New York Review of Books*, XIV, No. 4 (Feb. 26, 1970), 34.

24. Wayne C. Booth, *The Rhetoric of Fiction* (Chicago: The University of Chicago Press, 1961), p. 120.

25. Booth, pp. 119-20.

the true origins, the true motives or the truth about life itself."[26]
Those critics, says Booth, who study the third perspective are concerned with the qualitative value of the work: "We have, or can be
made to have, a strong desire to see any pattern or form completed, or
to experience further development of qualities of any kind. We might
call this kind [of literary interest] 'aesthetic'."[27] Finally, according to
Booth, critics whose main interest is in the fourth perspective are concerned with the practical value of the work: "We have, or can be made
to have, a strong desire for the success or failure of those we love or
hate, admire or detest; or we can be made to hope for or fear a change
in the quality of a character. We might call this kind [of literary inter-
est] 'human'."[28] In terms of Booth's categories, I am concerned in this
study with works as they affect readers, the main focus being on the
practical side, the "human" side of reader emotional response to character.

The cognitive basis of my critical approach is both existential and
psychological. An existential perspective on a work rests on the belief
that there is no absolute essence deep within a work: the essence of the
work is, rather, within each individual reader. Although this kind of
statement may sound like a meaningless juggling of words, it is important to note that the shift of emphasis from the idea of truth within the
work to truth within the reader calls for a critical perspective which
differs basically from that of traditional criticisms. The three critical
approaches, briefly delineated above, imply to some extent that there is
an absolute meaning within the work — an essence which partisan critics hope to elucidate through intellectual recognition. Yet, underlying
the factors which lead to intellectual recognition is the dynamic process
through which the reader relates to the work, to the emotive substance
wherein feelings are registered by the writer and aroused in the reader.
Through the dynamics of feelings, readers continually re-interpret and
"re-create" the text in context with their individual experiences, as well
as in the context of milieu and culture. Susanne Langer says that a
major purpose of a work of art is to objectify the life of feeling.[29]
Underlying this idea is her statement that the spectrum of emotions is

26. Booth, p. 125.
27. Booth, p. 125.
28. Booth, p. 125.
29. Susanne K. Langer, *Feeling and Form: A Theory of Art* (New York: Charles
Scribner's Sons, 1953), p. 374.

the organizing "idea" in the temporal and non-temporal arts.[30] The perception of feelings, of course, belongs to the intellectual domain of conceptualization and symbolization. But the reader also experiences feelings while he is reading; such an experience is related to the realm of biological event/emotion. J. F. Rychlak, in *A Philosophy of Science for Personality Theory,* generalizes: "Everyone knows that an emotion is, among other things, a physical reaction of some sort, that it hinges in large measure upon body chemistry, and that it influences behavior in certain ways."[31] This aspect of human reaction is the basis for speaking of essence in the reader. In other words, by responding emotionally to a text, the reader creates a subjective life of feeling related to that which the author has objectified — he "re-creates" the work for himself. Within this context, one may say that reading literature is contingent upon a reader's other experiences in life. One might envision the reading experience by analogy. A stranger finds himself in a new and different land which he has sought out or where he arrives accidentally. The language, activities, customs, appearances of the people have an air of familiarity; at the same time, the new-comer is aware that he is encountering the aspects of life around him in a different configuration than ever before. Similarly, each individual will have different reactions to a text depending upon the things which make him a unique being. However, to speak of reader response to literature, one must go beyond the existential feature of uniqueness to find some base of commonality which will explain why great literature is characterized by standing outside time and space — by being so basically human as to allow readers centuries and continents apart to understand and relate to a given work. It is this mimetic quality of "universal" emotionality in great literary works that causes the reading of that work to be a dynamic experience for the reader. W. J. Harvey quotes the opinion given by Dr. Johnson in his "Preface to Shakespeare": "Imitations produce pain or pleasure, not because they're mistaken for realities, but because they bring realities to mind."[32]

To consider the common elements of literature, and thus in man, one must look at the psychological aspect of the critical approach used

30. Langer, p. 373.

31. Joseph F. Rychlak, *A Philosophy of Science for Personality Theory* (Boston: Houghton, Mifflin Co., 1968), pp. 366-67.

32. W. J. Harvey, *Character and the Novel* (London: Chatto and Windus, 1965), p. 215.

in this study. Certain "insights" in a twentieth century Western reader's view of human nature are attributable to modern psychology. Rousseau departed from Cartesian thought by giving emotion a place of importance equal to that of reason. In the same tradition, a basic tenet of modern psychology is the idea that man's feelings are not separable from his mental activity, and, in fact, that mind and feeling shape each other continually in every activity. A second tenet of modern psychology is the idea that the formation and expression of individual feelings is inextricably linked to one's daily experiences with family, friends, and society. Although it is not necessary that one agree with the factual value of these statements, they do express attitudes subtly incorporated into twentieth century Western thought about man and his behavior. In Eric Auerbach's estimation:

> Ever since its beginnings in Greece, European literature has possessed the insight that a man is an indivisible unity of body (appearance and physical strength) and spirit (reason and will), and that his individual fate follows from that unity . . . . 20th-century psychology has both added to and clarified the above "insight". Man is body and mind, but man is also feeling and motivation. Man's acts and thoughts are primarily governed by a vast substructure of subconscious motivations. Viewed from this perspective, mind and body – thought and act are united – no longer are we puzzled by the observable gap between desire and deed, thought and act, the real and the ideal – for once we understand what motivates man, the gaps are explainable.[33]

Auerbach speaks of a "vast substructure of subconscious motivations." This study is not concerned with the unconscious of the author or reader. Rather, an interest in the dynamic aspect of the text will consider how feeling readers relate to the feelings implicit in a literary work of art. Thus, psychological theory used here will consist of general referrals to basic psychological concepts about emotional reactions, as opposed to detailed, categorical use of psychoanalytic constructs. But, before talking about the nature of literary response, it will be useful to return for a moment to the philosophical (existential) base of the critical perspective.

In discussing the shift in focus from the traditional idea of truth in the text to the idea of truth in the reader, it was suggested that the work itself becomes, from a psychological viewpoint, a dynamic repository of recorded feelings as well as of ideas. Within the context of an

---

33. Eric Auerbach, *Dante Poet of the Secular World*, trans. by Ralph Manheim (Chicago: The University of Chicago Press, 1961), pp. 1-2.

existential interpretation, the literary work can be considered, if one accepts Doubrovsky's definition, as, "la somme des réponses possibles aux questions réelles que se posent un homme et à travers lui, une époque, une civilisation et à la limite l'humanité."[34] Although question and response belong to the realm of cognition, it is also feasible to say that a person feels one way when he is thinking about a question and another way when he finds a response. These feelings can be called conflict/resolution. On the emotional level, conflict implies a sense of being suspended, uncertain, searching; resolution suggests relaxation, relief, momentary certainty. Bringing this into the domain of literature, it is generally known that great works of art reflect tension to some degree both in form and in content. Susanne Langer has expressed the opinion that all the arts exhibit "an interplay of what artists in every realm call 'tensions'."[35] Character confrontations, linguistic obscurities, situational obstacles — this is the language of literature — the ingredients of the complexity of which life itself is made. In *Homo Ludens,* Huizinga observes that, "the writer's aim, conscious or unconscious, is to create a tension that will 'enchant' the reader and hold him spellbound. Underlying all creative writing is some human or emotional situation potent enough to convey this tension to others."[36] Thus the artist reflects conflicts while providing resolutions. Frederick Crews corroborates the idea that "the artist has the power to sublimate and neutralize conflict, to give it logical and social coherence through conscious elaboration and to reach and communicate a sense of catharsis."[37] Then, if there is tension expressed on the intellectual level (question/response) and on the emotional level (conflict/resolution), a work viewed from this perspective might be described as a pattern of rhythms. On the one hand is the discursive rhythm of question and/or response: prose fiction is made up of language and ideas where one finds social, moral, philosophical meaning in a work. On the other hand, linked to the discursive rhythm is the non-discursive rhythm pattern of feeling. Of this aspect of a work, Doubrovsky says: "La littérature, c'est l'universel concret, l'homme non dans la clarté de son

34. Doubrovsky, p. 93.
35. Langer, p. 370.
36. Johan Huizinga, *Homo Ludens: A Study of the Play-Element in Culture* (Boston: The Beacon Press, 1950), p. 132.
37. Frederick Crews, "Literature and Psychology," p. 80.
38. Doubrovsky, p. 77.

intellect, mais dans l'opacité et la brutalité de ses passions."[38] The interplay of question/response on the intellectual level with the conflict/resolution aspect on the emotional level creates and sustains the tensions which characterize form and content, and it is through this feeling of tension (intellectual/emotional) that the reader feels drawn into a work or draws the work into himself. However, the degree to which a reader feels conflict/resolution (anxiety/relief) depends on his personal experiences and the strength of his own emotivity, as well as on the content and form of the work itself.

Since emotional response to a work varies from reader to reader, so much so that a discussion of a work in terms of the specific emotions it engenders would be meaningless, one can only speak with reference to basic tensions in a work and corollary tensions in man. Although the causes of tensions are unique to each person, the fundamental feelings produced may conform to commonly recognizable patterns of reaction such as tears or laughter. Rollo May asks: "Does not every human conflict reveal universal characteristics of man as well as the idiosyncratic problems of the individual? "[39] One may propose, then, that at the question/conflict level of reading, the reader feels some degree of uncertainty, or if one may use a psychological term, anxiety, although the anxiety experienced while reading will probably be only the slight irritation of doubt or puzzlement. Traditional literary criticism deals readily with the tension (anxiety) element in a work; yet, many critics do not often focus on the corollary pattern of tension in the reader. Frederick Crews takes exception to criticism which he feels misleads the reader by denying that the author expresses in his work his own tensions and anxieties:

> All literary criticism aims to make the reading experience more possible for us, but anaesthetic criticism assumes that this requires keeping caged the anxieties that the artist set free and then recaptured. The effect is often to transform the artist from a struggling fellow mortal into an authority figure, a dispenser of advice about virtue and harmony.[40]

In keeping with Crews' judgment, one will consider, for the moment, Rabelais's books as reflections of his intellectual and emotional self as

39. Rollo May, *Love and Will* (New York: W. W. Norton & Co., Inc., 1969), p. 19.

40. Frederick Crews, "Anaesthetic Criticism: II," pp. 49-52 in *The New York Review of Books,* XIV, No. 5 (March 12, 1970), 50.

well as of the intellectual/emotional currents in his society. More specifically, Panurge will be viewed as symbolic of the implicit tensions.

Critics in the Cartesian tradition, have described Panurge as symbolic of philosophical doubt; others have rationally discussed his character traits of childishness, cowardliness, insecurity. Obviously, these descriptions all characterize Panurge. If one goes one step further, it is feasible to say that insofar as Panurge may represent the state of emotional transition from childhood to adulthood, a period fraught with multiple tensions, he embodies the concepts of uncertainty, anxiety, and ultimately the principle of emotion itself, if one accepts the hypothesis that "feeling and emotion are really complexes of tension."[41] It might be suggested that to the degree that Panurge portrays emotions associated with growing up, he expresses tensions common to everyone in varying degrees. By posing questions, Panurge is seeking intellectual responses; by bearing the weight of uncertainties and anxieties, he looks for emotional resolutions. The sought after response need be only a possible answer, a temporary solution to the question/conflict, to provide Panurge and the reader with a feeling of relief, of relaxation. The emotional effect associated with relief would be happiness, a kind of momentary security.

Before studying Panurge in more detail, it might prove useful to examine the parts played by form and content in the process of reader response. Although there are numerous critical treatments of form (style and genre) and its components (language, imagery, symbol), little has been said about the emotional aspects of form in terms of their effects on the reader. In psychological terms, the form of a literary work has been compared to means which an individual uses to adapt to his life situation.[42] In other words, the author presents his vision of life

---

41. Langer, p. 74.

42. Norman Holland expresses his opinion about the "defensive" function of literary form: "From a psychological point of view ... the terms "defense" or "adaptation" do not quite fit .... This kind of transformation does not correspond exactly to a defense, for a defense is an unconscious mechanism of the ego that comes into play automatically at a signal of danger. The plot in a story does serve as a way of handling dangers; but it is not unconscious, nor is it automatic. By contrast, an adaptation is more autonomous than automatic and goes beyond the mere resolution of conflicts toward progressive, constructive, and maturational mastery of drives. A plot resembles adaptation in being more autonomous than automatic, but there is no guarantee that a plot — or any other transformational device

within a genre and in a style harmonious with his own knowledge, experiences and feelings and in this way somewhat controls the intellectual and emotional stances which the readers will take toward his vision of life. Simon O. Lesser thinks that in regard to the reader, form has three essential functions in narrative art: (1) to give pleasure in and of itself; (2) to facilitate perception – to silhouette the material with the desired degree of clarity; (3) to relieve anxiety.[43] While the first two attributes of form are familiar to traditional criticism, the third attribute which is related to the "affective" side of literary experience is not often considered. Lesser clarifies the third function of form, explaining that the anxiety aroused in the reader by the tension in the content of the work, is paralleled, enhanced and controlled by the form. Of course, readers will relate differently to form, depending on the nature of their own defensive adaptations. For example, the reader who adjusts to life by trying to find humor in situations will probably respond more readily to the intellectual/emotional rhythms of Rabelais than to those of Racine.

The tension expressed and controlled by form is at the same time manifested both directly and indirectly, consciously and unconsciously, in the content of the work, through themes. "Theme" might be defined as a cognitive name given to recognizable ideas, feelings, and fantasies in the work. Traditional criticism tends to emphasize the intellectual components in feelings and fantasies found in a work of literary art. In keeping with the focus on reader emotional response to the emotive substance in a work, this study will stress the significance of fantasy within the context of the dynamic process of literary emotional response. Initially, the concern is with the basic process of "fantasizing;" subsequently, the cognitive content of the specific fantasies will be considered.

in literature – moves in the direction of maturation .... In short, to describe psychologically the combination of agents of transformation in a literary work, we need a generic psychological term that does not exist: for something that is not necessarily in and of itself adaptive, but can add up to a kind of adaptation; for something that looks like such well-known defenses as regression, isolation, reversal, and the like, although it is not an unconscious, automatic psychic mechanism like them but rather an explicit handling of an implicit fantasy." Norman N. Holland, *The Dynamics of Literary Response* (New York: Oxford University Press, 1968), pp. 105-06.

43. Simon O. Lesser, *Fiction and the Unconscious* (New York: Random House Inc., 1962), p. 125.

Although traditional criticism discusses the fantasy element in fiction, many critics seem to find this element a bit distasteful. The reason for this is, possibly, a failure on the part of those critics to grasp the full impact of what fantasy means psychologically. Simon Lesser expresses the opinion that empirical studies of response to fiction suggest that the fear of investigating the fantasy component in a narrative work has two basic sources. First, fantasies are feared because of their wishful nature. The wishes may be feared on their own account and because they arouse ideas of punishment and retaliation. The wish component entails the ideas of both childish egotism and forbidden impulses. Secondly, another basis of fear is suggested by the ambiguity of the phrase "to tell a story;" it is the fear of confusing fiction and reality, reality and truth.[44] However, when "fantasy" is mentioned in this study, it will not refer to a reader's wishful identification with a beautiful, rich, successful character or with an adventurous, exciting situation, although such identifications certainly occur. Rather, one is concerned with *essential* fantasies shared to some degree by human beings and stemming from basic, physiological, emotional nature. In a broad, somewhat primitive sense, one refers to fantasies issuing from sexual feelings, from hostile feelings, from anxieties. Obviously, it is not plausible to speak of commonality in specific fantasy content for this is determined and limited by the period, the culture, and the uniqueness of the individual.

A standard dictionary definition of the psychological meaning of "fantasy" is, "an imaginative sequence, especially one in which desires are fulfilled; daydream."[45] As implied in this definition, the agent by which the individual fantasizes is the imagination. A standard dictionary definition of the psychological meaning of "imagination" is, "the power of reproducing images stored in the memory under the suggestion of associated images or of recombining former experiences to create new images."[46] Then, the imagination has at its command, remembrance of past experience, thoughts, and feelings. Depending on current needs and desires, an individual may create an imagined situation which may be set in the past, present, or future — a fantasy. To fantasize, that

44. Lesser, p. 6.
45. *The Random House Dictionary of the English Language: College Edition,* Laurence Urdang, Editor in Chief (New York: Random House, Inc., 1968), p. 478.
46. *The Random House Dictionary of the English Language,* p. 663.

is, to wish for something to be different from what it is or appears to be, involves setting into motion a mental apparatus in the service of the feelings. Although one cannot generalize about feelings which generate wishes, a feeling preceding a wish may range from the need or desire to change the most basic physiological state (hunger, thirst, etc.) to a complex, grandiose desire to change one's life style. One can, however, generalize about the physio-psychological nature of feelings, and by extention, of wishes. If one accepts Langer's description of feelings as complexes of tensions, a wish may be said either to reduce existing tensions (calm feelings) or to create added tension (stir up feelings); thus a wish may produce conflict or resolution. On the premise that a wish may create an emotional state of conflict and/or resolution, one might suggest the following analogy: the process of wishing (fantasizing) is dynamically related to the emotions (conflict/resolution) in the same manner that the process of doubting is dynamically related to the mind (question/response).

S. O. Lesser suggested two reasons, already cited, for a general distasteful reaction to the mention of the fantasy component in literature: the egotistical, forbidden nature of the wish or fantasy and the fear of confusing fiction and reality. Yet. if one views wishing not just as escapism, but, rather, as a basic physio-psychological process experienced by all people to varying degrees, the process becomes a bit more acceptable. For the period of time during which the wish (fantasy) is sustained, fiction is confused with reality; wishing is a willful mingling of reality and unreality in order to fulfill some feeling, be it a pleasant memory from the past or the setting of the stage for some future action. Psychologist B. G. Rosenberg adheres to this view of fantasy:

> Fantasy may be compensatory, but we must realize that it also is an integrative function. Fantasy is fulfilling as a process, as well as being a vehicle for the contents of conflict resolution.[47]

While reading, an individual relates simultaneously in two different ways to the fantasy aspect of a fictional work. On an intellectual level he judges and analyzes what the fiction means to him, aware that although fiction means "unreal", it does not necessarily mean "untrue". Elizabeth Janeway has recently restated this idea which has previously been expressed by many author-critics:

---

47. B. G. Rosenberg, "Psychology Through the Looking Glass," pp. 55-56 and 68 in *Psychology Today*, V, No. 1 (June, 1971), 56.

Unfortunately, it's characteristic of the present age to hold "fiction" synony-mous with "untrue". This isn't so. Good fiction is always concentrated truth, or the apotheosis of fact by the discovery therein of a living, active drive to be-come − a process trying to enunciate a principle which will survive until it, in turn, is falsified because it no longer expresses true feelings.[48]

Secondly, a reader experiences a work emotionally, as he perceives it intellectually. In a psychological analysis of this process, Norman Hol-land paraphrases the poet Coleridge:

It is precisely our conscious knowledge that we are dealing with unreality that makes it possible for us to relax, to suspend our disbelief, and in a way to respond to the unreality as though it were real. Conversely, during the time we think the fiction is real, we are tense, sometimes even to the point of displeas-ure . . . . The inactivity involved in our willing suspension of disbelief . . . . per-mits . . . a sort of total immersion in fantasy.[49]

Obviously, a reader will not experience the same emotional response toward a fantasy created by someone else (the author) that he will experience toward a fantasy of his own creation. One expects fantasy in fiction; one expects that the fantasy elements will be "controlled" for him. Nonetheless, the combined experience of intellectually judging the fantasy elements of fiction while having personal feelings about the basic fantasies described is one of the reasons that readers respond to certain literary works of art. The reader finds himself, as Joyce Cary has suggested, in a fairly recognizable world of concentrated truths and feelings:

Only art can convey both the fact and the feeling about the fact, for it works in the medium of common sympathies, common feeling, universal reaction to col-our, sound, form. It is the bridge between souls, meaning by that not only men's minds but their character and feeling.[50]

In the ensuing study of Panurge, "fantasy" refers to the themes through which the characters convey wishes and feelings which may be aroused in the reader. To the degree that the fantasy expresses recognizable wishes and feelings, it shall be considered "real".

One fantasy syndrome with which modern psychology and philo-sophical existentialism has familiarized the twentieth century Western

48. Elizabeth Janeway, "Happiness and the Right to Choose," pp. 118-26 in *Atlantic Monthly*, March, 1970, p. 118.

49. Holland, p. 68 and p. 72.

50. Joyce Cary, *Art and Reality: Ways of the Creative Process* (Garden City, New York: Anchor Books, Doubleday & Co., Inc., 1961), pp. 22-23.

world centers around thoughts and feelings about freedom and security. This particular theme is appropriate because it is central to the interpretation of Panurge presented in this study. From earliest childhood the individual rebels to varying degrees against the restrictions of parents, school, and society. At the same time that a person desires to be free of restrictions, there tends to be a simultaneous wish to be protected, cared for, made secure. Throughout a lifetime, as individuals continue to seek countless freedoms and securities, many of them incompatible, conflicts and anxieties often arise out of the inconsistencies. It is not, then, surprising that a repetitive theme in great Western literature deals with the individual "against" authority, freedom versus conformity, doubt versus certainty, insecurity versus security. When one reads a work which deals with these themes, he may well modify his own fantasies surrounding questions of freedom and security through form, language, themes, and character confrontations, to meaning. The reader clothes his feelings in stylistic, intellectual, philosophical garments, and thus orders and organizes his emotional tensions. Yet, he continues to relive his basic fantasies, intellectually by analogy and emotionally through imagination. It is not that the reader becomes the characters about whom he is reading; it is not that he actually believes himself to be in the literary situation. It is, rather, that he undergoes a symbolic process of self-confrontation.[51] According to Frederick Crews, "we are invited, not to experience a fantasy, but to share a posture toward [our own feelings]."[52]

Panurge is the character who expresses what this study will call the essential fantasy in Rabelais — the desire for free expression pitted against a search for certain security. Thematically, this fantasy is developed as Panurge's quest for marriage. He longs for a wife but is afraid of being duped; he wishes to be a part of the adult-world, but refuses to accept responsibility. Panurge's desire for a sense of security which he simultaneously shuns creates in him a tension which leaves him anxious, uncertain, confused. Intellectually, Panurge's dilemma suggests the age-old quest for philosophical "Truth"; emotionally, his plight is that of the individual seeking certainty and security in a chaotic, uncertain world.

Form and language fluctuate in much the same manner as Panurge's

51. Crews, "Anaesthetic Criticism: II," p. 51.
52. Crews, "Anaesthetic Criticism: II," p. 52.

feelings and fantasies. Passages of clear, straight-forward prose are followed by chapters of nonsensical, linguistic frenzy. The reader is told that life is only for laughing and drinking; the biting satire intertwined with this advice leaves the reader wondering if things are after all as funny as they are said to be. In this major character, form and language combine to express confusion, uncertainty. Rather than dismiss the turmoil by saying with M. A. Screech that all of Rabelais has not yet been deciphered, or by saying that it is not really an important part of the books, might one not accept that this feeling is implicit in the texture of the work? Hopefully, some further intellectual understanding of Rabelaisian uncertainty can be gained by looking at Panurge as an emotional entity who expresses feelings and fantasies which are as important to an understanding of Rabelais's work as a whole as are the philosophical meanings attributed to this character's existence in the work.

CHAPTER II: LITERARY CHARACTER –
PANURGE, EMOTION-IN-ACTION

Literary character, Panurge specifically, is the vantage point from which this study will consider reader emotional response to a fictional work of literature. Throughout recorded history, those interested in the study of literature have posed the question, "What is character? " and have answered it variously, thereby reflecting the views of a given society and age on "personality" as well as suggesting certain immutable aspects of what literary character is. Traditional criticism has tended toward views about fictional character that modern critics might label simplistic. Characters, according to traditionally oriented critics, are imitations of other literary characters or of real people, are portraits of existing types of people or are projections of the author's imagination. Most modern critics tend to interpret character as a combination of all these. My study will consider another dimension of character study which is of fairly recent interest to literary critics: character is also a medium through which central tensions in a work are expressed, that is, a receptacle for the emotional dynamics of the work. Another way to phrase this idea is, "Character is the driving force in fiction."[1]

There is a current tendency for many literary critics to regard character study as uninteresting. W. J. Harvey suggests several reasons for this. Some critics tend to see character studies as morally unhealthy because they encourage the reader to fantasize and to identify wrongly with the hero or heroine. Secondly, Harvey says, there is the fear that character studies may allow the critic to evade the proper task of criticism and formation of value judgments by offering mere descriptive sketches of character. Thirdly, character studies often operate on the basis of general concept which posits fixed character types or on the basis of abstract concept which views character as projection of the author's imagination or unconscious. Neither general nor abstract concepts of character take into account the concrete experience of a book:

---

1. Leon Surmelian, *Techniques of Fiction Writing: Measure and Madness* (Garden City, New York: Doubleday and Company, Inc., 1968), p. 139.

Fourth, character studies seem to ignore the real object of criticism which is to try to understand the moral vision of the artist as manifested in a particular and concrete pattern of words. Fifth, character studies deflect attention from the unity of the total work to see the part as larger than the whole. For example, a character study might take into account Hamlet the prince rather than *Hamlet* the play. Sixth, character studies tend to deny the autonomy of the created artifact and confuse real emotions with aesthetic emotions.[2] Finally, many authors discourage character study by propagating the attitude that literary characters are mysterious *données*.[3]

One might divide these criticisms into two categories. The idea that reading a work of literature is only an aesthetic experience and should never be confused with an emotional experience is expressed in the first and sixth reasons given for avoiding character study. As noted in chapter I, this study rejects the idea that reading is only an aesthetic endeavor. The other five critisms of character study have to do generally with the idea that at its best character study is good description which nonetheless does not fulfill the critical task, or that, at its worst, it attempts to be analytical but fails because it does not bridge the gap between character itself and the relation of character to the work as a whole and to the reading experience. As already proposed, character is not separate from the work as a whole. Rather, character may be intricately and necessarily woven into the texture of the work. Thus character expresses and is expressive of style, content, themes, imagery and ultimately is the purveyor of the intellectual and emotional rhythms of the author's vision. From this perspective, character becomes a viable and even necessary focus for serious literary criticism.

One further reason for a lack of interest in character study has to do with the fact that since the end of the nineteenth century there has been a vast amount of experimentation with technical aspects of fiction writing. Critics have kept pace with writers's experimentations by themselves analyzing narrative technique, symbolization, thematics, structural principles and systems and so forth. As a consequence, very little that can be considered "new" has been said about character, the traditional

---

2. W. J. Harvey, *Character and the Novel* (London: Chatto and Windus, 1965), p. 206.
3. Harvey, p. 196.

mainstay of fiction, since E. M. Forster's analysis of character in *Aspects of the Novel* written in 1927.[4]

Accepting that character study is a worthwhile critical task, one must examine more thoroughly the critical basis for the idea that character is a medium through which central tensions in a work are expressed. Two basic critical orientations were discussed in the first chapter: the text seen as autonomous whole created only for the reader's aesthetic pleasure (Northrop Frye, José Ortega y Gasset); the text viewed in the mimetic tradition which sees no final discontinuity between the reader's responses to art and to life (W.J. Harvey). Probably the difference between these two orientations is one of degree and not of kind. On one level the reader deals intellectually with ideas and stylistics (the aesthetic view); simultaneously, the reader experiences the text emotionally (the mimetic view). Within a mimetic perspective, one does not merely have a reading experience; one is the reading experience and the work is the reader's experience of it.[5] While aesthetic theory derives from an emphasis on the intellectual components of a text wherein truth and beauty result from a combination of all the elements of fiction formed by the *Je ne sais quoi* of the creator's genius, mimetic theory brings the elements of the work, the author's genius and the reader's experience of the work, down from the realm of the transcendent to the arena of real, concrete experience. One sees the artist writing out of his struggle with life and the reader relating concretely to the struggle. And the struggle is seen as an *a priori* premise of living. It must be admitted, however, that it is precarious to attempt a mimetic theory insofar as the texture of life is infinitely varied and liable to rapid historical change. Consequently, the only viable terms for a mimetic view of the reading experience are within the framework of a basic

---

4. Harvey, pp. 192 and 194.

5. To clarify further the mimetic view of the reading experience, it is worthwhile to cite a comment made about the ideas of existential psychologist, Harry S. Sullivan: "What we are asked to accept [by Harry S. Sullivan] is that in quite a real sense the self [reader] is one's personal relationships. We have tended in the past to suppose that we are self-contained individuals looking out from a tower in our own private castle from which we proceed on periodic excursions in order to satisfy physical, emotional and mental needs and desires. We assumed that our contacts with the world left us relatively untouched, the same person as before. In the opinion of Sullivan this is a complete fallacy. We do not merely have experiences — we are experiences." J. A. C. Brown, *Freud and the Post-Freudians* (Baltimore, Maryland: Penguin Books, 1967), p. 166.

structure of experience: conflict/resolution = tension.[6] One might even propose that certain literary prose works evolve as classics in the degree that basic tensions of the human condition are eludicated both in form and in content. From this perspective one could say that good fiction is inseparable from good characters if one accepts the proposal that the basic tensions in a work are portrayed by the characters. Good fiction is thus defined as representing the real texture of the life of the most basic human feelings. According to Surmelian, "Successful characters are people-in-tension, if not always people-in-action."[7]

However, not all "good" literary characters express the complexity of the basic tensions of the emotional life rhythm. For example, there are generally two types of characters said to be without tension, one-dimensional: farcical, stock characters and allegorical figures. Insofar as Panurge is on one level a farcical, stock character, this kind of character will be discussed at some length in the following discussion of what makes character real. Allegorical characters will only be briefly mentioned for they are not relevant here. Allegorical figures do not enter the domain of emotion; it might even be said that these figures are the antithesis of emotion, of tension. The complexities of feelings have been drained away leaving a residue of character seen as intellectual abstraction about emotion. Consequently, these figures seem to personify just one quality.[8]

Three areas should be probed further before Panurge is analyzed. What is character in terms of the work as a whole? How does the reader know character? What makes character real? One may answer the first question by positing character as a link bewteen the form and content of the work. For example, comedies have some comic characters. One can also say that character is a link between the author's vision and the reader's perception of that vision. An artist's special gift is his ability to integrate the perceptual and the conceptual, to make his thoughts and feelings seem almost visually perceivable.[9] The agents of this visual perception are the characters in a fictional work. Harvey finds character so important to a consideration of the whole of a work that he asks, "What do we care for theme or for moral vision, except

6. Harvey, p. 23.
7. Surmelian, p. 148.
8. Surmelian, p. 144.
9. René Wellek and Austin Warren, *Theory of Literature* (New York: Harcourt, Brace and World, Inc., 3rd ed., 1962), p. 83.

insofar as these are incarnated in human realities? In our response to and our exploration of those we extend and explore ourselves."[10] Finally, one can say that character serves as a link between author and reader because he is emotion-in-action.[11]

In answer to the question "How does one know character? " it might be said that a reader knows character both directly and indirectly. Directly, "objectively", the reader observes the character's overt behavior and thus knows him by his words, acts and interactions with other characters. Indirectly, "subjectively", the reader interprets the meaning of a character's behavior in the context of his own experiences, thoughts, feelings and fantasies; mimetically speaking, character is an emotional extension of the reader himself. Yet, to say merely that a reader knows character objectively and subjectively is to simplify the process.

Psychoanalytic critical studies have considered the relationship between reader and literary character and have concluded that the reader knows character through a process in which he satisfies individual drives vicariously by identifying with the literary character.[12] In psychoanalytic terms this so-called identification, "making oneself the same as,"[13] is a complicated mixture of projection and introjection, of taking in from the character certain drives and defenses that are really objectively "out here" and of putting into him feelings that are really one's own, "in here".[14] This kind of study seems to present some major difficulties. First, the factors involved in reader identification with character are too subjective and too varied for the critic to treat except in a most general manner. Secondly, an emphasis on the psychoanalytic dynamics of character recognition may fail to take into account the importance of character to the work as a whole. Although psychoana-

10. Harvey, p. 211.

11. Harvey views character as the "visual" embodiment of emotion: "The defined emotion gives the writer not only a motive, a subject, a theme, but also the action . . . . An emotion is not a stationary force, it is a tumultuous movement, and it gives movement to the plot. It is not diffuse, aimless, ending nowhere, but it is definite and channeled, canalizing the action it instigates. The emotion "insists" on realizing its end. It has a goal, but its goal . . . is frustrated, and if fiction is to be true to life it must depict frustrated emotions." Harvey, p. 94.

12. Norman N. Holland, *The Dynamics of Literary Response* (New York: Oxford University Press, 1968), p. 278.

13. Holland, p. 262.

14. Holland, p. 278.

lysts and critics are constantly learning more about the process of identification, this study will only examine the tensions basic to the work as
a whole which are manifested through character rather than examining
the dynamics of character "re-creation" through projection and introjection. In treating so delicate an issue as reader response, one must
speak in terms of basics, both in the text and in the reader.

As mentioned in the first chapter, a central tension in Rabelais's
work focuses on a consideration of absolute's versus relativity. More
concretely, the reader sees the tensions implicit in such an abstract
problem expressed by the dilemma of the character Panurge; thus the
reader knows Panurge by relating to the emotional tension inherent in
the human process of decision-making. The theme which develops Panurge's indecisiveness is symbolically most appropriate: should one
marry or not? Translated into other terms the question becomes:
should one accept responsibility? should one pay his debts? should
one take the emotional risk of failure? And in creating a character who
cannot resolve this problem Rabelais magnifies a basic human tension
to resounding, epic proportions. Indecisive Panurge is expressive of the
existential reality of the human condition. Free to do whatever he
wishes, for all choices are open to him, he is nonetheless imprisoned in
his inability to make a decision for fear that it might not be the right
decision. Given this paradox, it is not surprising that there is a critical
debate about whether or not Panurge is a free person. However, to
make of Panurge an existential "hero" is not the purpose of this study.
One may take another viewpoint concerning the metaphorical meaning
of Panurge's indecisiveness. Twentieth century psychologists say that in
growing from childhood to adulthood a child should be taught how to
make his own decisions. In a manner of speaking, the child must become his own parent. To the extent that a person does not learn to
make his own decisions, to act on them and to accept responsibility for
them, this person remains emotionally a child, unfree.

It must be noted, however, that the tensions implicit in making
decisions, in becoming independent, are much more extreme in some
societies than in others. For example:

> Japanese parents encourage dependency as actively as American parents push
> independence, and ... healthy children and adults in Japan rely heavily on
> others for emotional support and decisions about their lives.[15]

15. Philip Slater, *The Pursuit of Loneliness: American Culture at the Breaking
Point* (Boston: Beacon Press, 1970), p. 20.

In the Western world, nonetheless, becoming independent is a concept which is part of the cultural heritage. One does not need to accept twentieth century psychological theories of behavior to realize that the theme of revolt is a significant idea, for Western mythology and literature is illustrative of this fact. Obviously, every individual does not revolt in a grandiose manner, yet the tension resulting from having to choose among alternatives is a physiological reality. Although in Rabelais's society a person probably did not have the range of decisions to make that he has in the twentieth century, the sixteenth century in France was, nonetheless, an age marked by religious, economic and political changes, thus opening avenues to wider possibilities of personal choice and concomitant uncertainty than existed in the Middle Ages where the structures of Catholic Church and feudal society greatly determined an individual's life.

In discussions of revolt and potential freedom, twentieth century psychologists and philosophers agree on one point — total freedom, which implies omnipotence and possible anarchy, is unattainable in human experience. Yet to the degree that one can make his own decisions and accept the responsibilities inherent in the act of choosing, he is more free than he might otherwise be: "Freedom abides in our ability to choose."[16] Panurge's indecisiveness, his relative impotence, make of him a prototype of the existential tension within man, a prototype of the child within man. By sustaining Panurge's indecision throughout three books Rabelais maintains reader interest in the character and in the work. The reader is emotionally awaiting the resolution of a conflict, although he is intellectually aware that the author is indicting the concept of absolute truth. Since Panurge does not make decisions, alternatives are perpetually open for him. The emotional rhythm conveyed to the reader is one of the illusion of being free, of controlling the outcome of the situation. As the reader "re-creates" his own thoughts, feelings and fantasies about freedom, he links himself to the tension element in the work which surrounds this particular theme:

> The freedom to choose between alternative possibilities of action puts man under a tremendous moral responsibility, but it is a creative responsibility both in life and in fiction .... Alternatives make for conflict, for drama, for complexity. Free will results in anxiety as well as in activity.[17]

16. Harvey, p. 131.
17. Surmelian, p. 152.

To know a character, in this context, is to respond to him as an emotional being, to the tension he expresses. This is the first step in the determination of what makes a given character real. That a character be real is central to a reader's responding to the character. Norman Holland clarfies this idea:

> The more clearly a given character embodies my tensions, the more the work of art stimulates those tensions in me: the more I have those tensions in myself anyway — why, then, the more real a given character will seem.[18]

In very broad terms it might be said that life is tension and death is resolution. A literary character who expresses tension can be seen as a living, dynamic creation. A real character, then, might be defined as a living picture while an unreal character is static, tensionless, emotionless. Yet one cannot say that every character who embodies a tension which the reader recognizes and feels is a real character. One may suggest that the tension expressed must take on an emotional charge which is inherent in the basic life rhythm. However, if one maintains that a character must manifest tension in order to be real, what becomes of farcical stock-type characters who are notably one-dimensional? More specifically, what becomes of Panurge?

In E. M. Forster's delineation of flat and round characters, three distinguishing features are attributed to the flat or "card" character: he often has an *idée fixe* or is constructed around a single quality;[19] he is not changed by circumstances;[20] he is not capable of surprising the reader.[21] Flat or one-dimensional characters are readily recognizable. They "never need re-introducing, never run away, have not to be watched for development."[22] These characters are also easily remembered by the reader afterwards: "They remain in his [the reader's] mind as unalterable for the reason that they were not changed by circumstances; they moved through circumstances, which gives them in retrospect a comforting quality, and preserves them when the book that produced them may decay."[23] The round character, on the other hand, does

---

18. Holland, p. 275.

19. E. M. Forster, *Aspects of the Novel* (New York: Harcourt, Brace and Company, 1927), pp. 103-04.

20. Forster, pp. 105-06.

21. Forster, p. 118.

22. Forster, p. 105.

23. Forster, pp. 105-06.

change; in his complexity he "waxes and wanes and has facets like a human being"[24]; he surprises the reader in a convincing way.[25]

Forster's analysis of character implies that round characters are real and that flat characters are not. Fittingly, heroes or protagonists are generally round while minor and comic characters are usually flat. Round characters, being complex, embody tensions that are similar to those felt by people in real life. Purely flat characters embody no tension for there is no complexity, no life-likeness. Yet, Forster's view of round and flat characters seems to neglect a basic point. Although purely flat characters do not embody tensions, they are nonetheless memorable which indicates that they can have a strong emotional impact on the reader. Implicit in this realization is the idea that if one is emotionally struck by a character, that character is by this very fact in some way real, life-like. One can, then, reverse Forster's proposal and suggest not only that flat characters may be as real as round ones, but possibly that they may be more so. In explanation of this statement one should consider various ways in which character is used to convey the basic tension of a work.

One technique presents a complex protagonist who reveals his story in the course of the work. His tensions are many or he experiences one tension profoundly. Various aspects of the tension or tensions expressed by the protagonist are reflected by characters other than the protagonist: "The definition of the emotion means the definition of the situation in which one or more people are involved. We know then what the problem is."[26] The responding reader, then, does not identify so much with a character as he does with a total interaction of characters in which some satisfy needs for pleasure and others satisfy needs to avoid anxiety.[27] Another technique through which tensions central to the work are expressed is one in which a protagonist consciously discusses the opposing forces of the tension. In this instance, the intellecting, philosophical reader is called into play. The hero, conscious of his dilemma, discusses it rationally, often crying out passionately against the conflicts involved in his plight. Even though this kind of hero may express profound emotional tensions, he does it intellectually, con-

24. Forster, p. 106.
25. Forster, p. 118.
26. Surmelian, p. 92.
27. Holland, p. 313.

sciously. The reader is led by genre, form, manner of characterization, to go to his own emotions through his mind, philosophically. Arthur Koestler synthesizes these various techniques: "The conflict may be fought in the divided heart of a single character; or between two or more persons; or between man and his destiny."[28]

Finally, tensions central to the work may be portrayed by minor characters as well as by the protagonist and major characters. Minor characters portray tensions when an *idée fixe,* which is symbolically a manifestation of their monolinearity, clashes with an obstacle, either a person or an idea, that refuses to yield before the obsession. This kind of character hits the reader forcibly as the vision of a single, strong, unconscious, emotion-in-action. Before the reader can think, he reacts by laughing, or grimacing or gesturing. An attribute of this kind of character is the given that no complexity is to be attributed to him; thus, the reader is not required to wait for the character to unveil himself. The reader is in control and may consequently feel or think what he wishes about this so-called simple character. According to W.J. Harvey, the realism of the flat character is "intensity, singleness, vivacity; the realism of the protagonist is that of dilution, complexity and process."[29]

In the first chapter it was stated that an implicit aspect of a literary reading experience is that the reader emotionally experiences the author's vision of life in context of his own emotional configuration. Within this perspective, a character who elicits a strong emotional response from the reader cannot be completely simple. Simple he may be in dimension. Yet if he elicits a real response, an emotional reaction from the reader, he has a certain complexity in that he is an extension of the reader himself: "This character then expresses a real part of our total complex of hopes, fears, etc."[30] The more profoundly a reader experiences the character, the better he knows that character and the more real the character seems. This proposed reversal of Forster's thesis about flat and round characters is, however, based on a consideration of reader "re-creation" only in the context of emotional recognition and identification. While the truly round character may be closer to the

28. Arthur Koestler, *The Act of Creation* (New York: Dell Publishing Company, Inc., 1967), p. 350.
29. Harvey, p. 62.
30. Harvey, p. 61.

complexity of reality, the truly flat character may elicit a more direct, more emotional reaction because he is immediately and easily graspable, seeable, knowable. Because of this the reader may understand him better, remember him longer, find him more real. For example, one may forget some of the intricacies of David Copperfield himself, but one never loses the vision of humble, obsequious Uriah Heep: "One great advantage of flat characters is that they are easily recognized whenever they come in — recognized by the reader's emotional eye, not by the visual eye, which merely notes the recurrence of a proper name."[31]

As mentioned, flat characters are usually considered to be types: they combine common traits and common problems which are so basic as to appear universal. Thus there is the hypocrite, the miser, the villain and so forth. Rarely, however, because of his nature, is a flat character taken seriously. He can neither grow nor change. Moreover, he seems to be swimming against the basic life current of growth and change. The first chapter refers to intellectual and emotional rhythms in a work of literature. Generally speaking, the specifics of growth and change belong first to the realm of intellectual rhythm. One can only grow and change by learning from instruction and from experience. In this context one may note the appeal of a hero to the intellect, to the sense of philosophical abstraction. On the other hand, the flat character appeals first to the feelings, to the emotional rhythm. Mary McCarthy comments that the reality of the "card" character is his incorrigibility and changelessness.[32] In agreement with many critics Miss McCarthy adds that most flat characters are comic. This perception is harmonious with Henri Bergson's thesis that people tend to laugh at whatever is rigid and changeless — a mechanical person or situation seen against the dynamic movement of the life rhythm causes one to laugh. Thus, the flat character with an *idée fixe,* with a limited vision of self and the world, makes the reader laugh. The reader laughs not only at the rigidity, the changelessness of the flat character, he laughs, as well, because this rigidity makes the character untameable. And, "The comic element is the incorrigible element in every human being."[33] Laughter itself is incorrigible if one views it as an outbreak of emotion over and above thought. In this context, one might expect a comic character to portray the essential emotional rhythm in a work.

31. Forster, p. 105.
32. Harvey, p. 59.
33. Harvey, p. 59.

Having discussed what character is, how one knows character and what makes character real, one must go further and pose the question of whether the character is convincing, believable. It is not sufficient to say that a character is real because the reader recognizes a common emotionality. To seem convincing a character must, in addition to expressing some emotional tension, be consistent.[34] Panurge is consistent throughout Rabelais's work in that he remains a stock-type character — the rogue, trickster of medieval tradition, the Cingar of the Italian burlesque poem. Were this the whole of the character there would be no puzzlement about his import. Yet on another level Panurge seems to be a pastiche of a real character, that is, a stock comic character with pretended real tensions and real emotions of indecision and fear. Unlike the typical farcical character type, Panurge even seeks to change or at least he gives lip-service to the idea of a quest that is supposed to help him resolve his problem.

Customary questions posed by critics about Panurge are: Who is he? Is he free? Is he unified? It is plausible to say that these questions can only be answered by a more basic one: Is Panurge a real character? If one does not question traditional criteria for realness of literary character, one will probably view Panurge as flat, comic, stock-type, unchanging, real-person-like, yet not real. On the other hand, one may say that Panurge is a real character on two counts. First, real people appear "flat" or "round" depending on how well one knows them. For example, one may know the postman only in his role of mail carrier. If one were to become personally acquainted with him, he would not be perceived as more real, only as less object-like, more complex — "round" rather than "flat". Panurge as comic character is indeed flat, graspable,

---

34. Surmelian explains the problem of consistency of literary character: "Characters would not be convincing if not consistent with themselves, or if inconsistent, consistently inconsistent. The inconsistency is a habit, like the caprices of some charming women; or reveals contradictions within the character. Does the character of the character change? Not much, if at all. There is a certain constancy of character in an eternally changing universe, and that is why we may say with Heraclitus that character is destiny. We are trapped by our characters. Every man is fated to be himself by a mysterious law of his own, and when we examine a life we shall probably find a basic continuity in it. Whether character is what a man does, or what a man is, an aggregate of his past acts and a sort of conditioned reflex or habit, or an intrinsic quality, independent of actions, not a legacy of the past, it has this self-consistent quality but is complex enough to surprise us on occasion. Actually no one is consistently consistent." Surmelian, pp. 145-46.

predictable, knowable. Rather than saying that this lack of complexity makes him unreal, not life-like, it might be said that, on the contrary, he is real as a type from whom one knows what to expect. In this view Panurge is consistent, unified in his sameness. Surmelian expresses the opinion that flat characters are characterized by a peculiar kind of freedom — the freedom of changelessness wherein they do not have to learn, grow or evolve, the freedom which lies in their immunity to the knocks and buffets doled out to them.[35] However, when one views Panurge's behavior from a psychological perspective and interprets him as child/man, he becomes more complex, less predictable, for one expects children to change and grow. From this perspective Panurge seems partially understandable as a "semi-round" character; secondly, then, he is real and consistent in a context different from that in which a flat character is real. The basis for realness herein is that of tensions expressed by Panurge and the reader's consequent emotional reaction to him. Thus Panurge is real insofar as he embodies tensions and fantasies common to readers throughout time and space.

It is possible that Panurge was first conceived as a stock-type character, as an imitation, but that Rabelais became so interested in him and invested so much of himself in this character that he actually became real.[36] Such an idea implies that character is not always consciously, logically developed. Perhaps, in some instances, the mimetic view of the reading experience might even be extended to the realm of character creation. The writer may experience and come to know a character as he creates him. Elizabeth Bowen says that characters pre-exist, that they are "found" by revealing themselves slowly to the writer's perception. And the writer's perception of his characters often takes place in the course of the actual writing. To the extent that this could be true,

35. Surmelian, p. 139.
36. In Surmelian's opinion, a "real" character expresses the emotional life rhythm and may attain this "reality" regardless of the writer's intention in creating him: "A writer knows when his characters come to life. Living characters display an astounding freedom and the author feels the continuous pull of their independence. They are irascible scene-stealers and threaten to run away with the show. Often they are secondary characters, not wearing the thematic strait jacket imposed on the hero, not obliged to prove anything. A writer is often more successful with his minor characters drawn directly from life and not burdened with the thematic responsibilities of the hero, and we usually remember these minor characters better than we remember the hero, especially if they are comical people." Surmelian, p. 148.

the writer is in the same position as the reader.[37] Then, according to Bowen, character is not created: "Better, the character is recognized by the signs he or she gives of unique capacity to act in a certain way, which 'certain way' fulfills a need of the plot."[38] In his analysis of Rabelais's creation of character, Glauser adheres to the view expressed by Bowen: "Les personnages sont des personnages en formation, se cherchant eux-mêmes, parce que leur auteur se cherche aussi et n'est pas sûr de ce qu'ils vont devenir. Ils sont les compagnons du créateur d'un roman qui s'écrit, qui se fait devant lui."[39]

Several characteristics may be attributed to Panurge in *Pantagruel* although they seem to fall into two rather general categories. On one hand, Panurge is a magnetic character described as jolly, joyful and fun-loving. At the same time, he is a rebel who controls his environment and his associates through cleverness, tricks, extreme confidence, boasting, exaggerations and lies. The reality of this Panurge is in his charm as a scene-stealer. Actually, he is a rogue who takes on the dimensions of a hero in terms of his affect but who certainly does not possess the traditional qualities of a hero. R. B. Heilman defines a rogue as one "who lives by his wits. The word 'rogue' suggests such other words as 'scamp' and 'rascal', the family of terms by which we designate the person who lives partly, though not threateningly, outside communal standards of responsibility."[40] The intellecting reader comes to know Panurge in the *Pantagruel* through his speech, actions and interactions as a character who behaves like the type called "rogue". That Panurge may be flat, comic character and rogue as well is not at all incompatible for, like the "card" character, the rogue is monolinear. "The key is shallowness."[41] However, from the subjective viewpoint of the emotional reader, the rogue takes on different dimensions. The rogue in and of himself is expressive of basic human fantasies. The rogue becomes symbolic as "the catharsis of rascality."[42] Through this character type

37. Elizabeth Bowen, "Notes on Writing a Novel," pp. 217-30 in *Perspectives on Fiction*, ed., James L. Calderwood and Harold E. Toliver (New York: Oxford University Press, 1968), p. 219.

38. Bowen, p. 219.

39. Alfred Glauser, *Rabelais créateur* (Paris: Editions A.-G. Nizet, 1966), p. 12.

40. Robert B. Heilman, "Felix Krull: Variations on Picaresque," pp. 101-09 in *Perspectives on Fiction*, ed., James Calderwood and Harold E. Tolliver (New York: Oxford University Press, 1968), p. 102.

41. Heilman, p. 103.

42. Heilman, p. 106.

the adult reader can imagine himself not limited to the confinements of actual self and of society; he may actively feel or unconsciously fantasize that he himself is clever enough to manipulate his environment and irresponsible enough to be free of the social rigors of work, laws and so forth. Therein lies much of the charm of the rogue for readers. From yet another perspective the rogue appeals to the not yet civilized man, to the child in man which lives "outside communal standards of responsibility."[43]

Panurge as real character, expressive of the child in each adult, is the subject of the next chapter. Further groundwork for this interpretation may be laid by viewing Panurge as representative of basic human fantasies of rebellion. One of the earliest physiological acts of each human being is to rebel by tears of rage against his own impotence and later to rebel by many and various means against the authorities that impose themselves against his will. Erik Erikson says:

> Every adult, whether he is a follower or a leader, a member of a mass or of an elite, was once a child. He was once small. A sense of smallness forms a substratum in his mind, ineradicably. His triumphs will be measured against this smallness, his defeats will substantiate it .... The unavoidable imposition on the child of outer controls which are not in sufficient accord with his inner control at the time, is apt to produce in him a cycle of anger and anxiety. This leaves a residue of an intolerance of being manipulated and co-erced beyond the point at which outer control can be experienced as self-control.[44]

Whether an individual's rebellious feelings are small or great, conscious or unconscious, realized or merely fantasized, they do exist and are ready to be tapped on an emotional level by a character such as the Panurge in *Pantagruel*. In a social context, to rebel against the norms is to risk feelings of doubt, fear, indecision. From this perspective it is not surprising that the egotistical, rebellious Panurge of *Pantagruel* becomes the doubting, uncertain questioner in *Le Tiers Livre*.

In the introduction to Panurge one is struck by the apparent yet unexplainable magnetism of the character. Before knowing anything of Panurge other than that he is in an impoverished state and that he was born and reared in Touraine, Pantagruel declares such a strong liking for him that he hopes he will never leave his side: "Doncques, dist Pantagruel, racomptez nous quel est vostre nom, et dont vous venez: car, par ma

43. Heilman, p. 102.
44. Erik H. Erikson, *Childhood and Society* (New York: W. W. Norton and Company, Inc., 1963), pp. 404 and 409.

foy, je vous ay ja prins en amour si grand que, si vous condescendez à mon vouloir, vous ne bougerez jamais de ma compaignie, et vous et moy ferons un nouveau pair d'amitié telle que feut entre Enée et Achates."[45] In chapter ix one learns that Panurge speaks several incomprehensible languages. On one level, Rabelais is playing another of his endless word games. On another level, one may suggest that Panurge is portrayed as a kind of enigma, a pre-figuration of the concept of "la sustantificque mouelle" of Rabelais's Prologue to *Gargantua*.[46] Curiosity, fascination of the unknown, are magnets for the human psyche. Thus, Panurge has already begun to manipulate Pantagruel and the reader by introducing himself as one who is outside the ordinary domain of the straightforward question/response level of communication. If he is to be known, he makes it clear from the start that he will be accepted on his terms whether or not those terms are ambiguous. In this initial meeting with Panurge, one also learns that he is an orphan with obscure origins and no fortune. In an age in which one's birthright was his passport, this renders Panurge even more mysterious. One wonders what the merits of his personality are that make this poor unknown so acceptable to wise, noble Pantagruel.

In chapter xvi the reader is told about Panurge's two major qualities: he is joyful and a trickster as well. The narrator describes him as "malfaisant, pipeur, beuveur, bateur de pavez, ribleur, s'il en estoit en Paris; au demourant, le meilleur filz du monde."[47] This rogue, this rebel, manipulates the world around him through his joy and his tricks, as well as through an excessive egotism which leads him to exaggerate his feats and powers, and finally through telling boldface lies. Except for the joy, the other qualities attributed to Panurge are generally considered undesirable character traits – the tools of the uncivilized, the misfit, the misanthrope. One may well ask how the normal reader could identify in fantasy with such a character. This is brought about by various means. First, Panurge is a comic character. His most sadistic tricks lose the appearance of being cruel because both the glee with which they are carried off and the humorous results tend to obscure the action itself. The humorous element creates an aura of light-hearted fun and unreali-

45. Rabelais, *Pantagruel, Oeuvres complètes*, vol. I, ed., Pierre Jourda (Paris: Editions Garnier Frères, 1962), p. 269.

46. Rabelais, *Gargantua, Oeuvres complètes*, vol. I, ed., Pierre Jourda (Paris: Editions Garnier Frères, 1962), p. 7.

47. Rabelais, *Pantagruel*, p. 301.

ty. Secondly, Panurge does possess some positive qualities. According to Heilman;

> The picaresque writer has the interesting technical problem of securing, for an extra-legal operator, "sympathy" and even "identification". He can do this by giving the [rogue] certain generally admired qualities – good nature, charm, an ironical view of himself or he can do it . . . by making the rogue somewhat a creature of necessity, maltreated by others and by circumstances.[48]

This quotation provides an excellent sketch of Panurge who is both a good-natured charmer and impoverished, tattered and lean from starvation. Thirdly, the reader may allow himself to identify with the rebellious nature of the rogue insofar as the rogue's victims do not steal any sympathy. The victims may be kept out of sight or they may get positive satisfaction from their dealings with the rogue or they may deserve what they get.[49] In Rabelais's work the treatment of Panurge's victims by the author is two-fold: either the victims are so lightly sketched as characters that no identification with them is possible or they symbolize satirical attacks against institutions and in this light get what they deserve. Finally, the reader is free to identify with the rogue both because his actions provide a kind of catharsis for floating hostilities and because this kind of character "appeals to a longing to reduce the muddled continuum of life to episodes manageable by cleverness alone."[50] The reader's attitude toward the rogue may be one of aloof superiority, or one of amusement, or one of shock, or one of actively cheering for the rogue. Whatever the reader's feeling and his resultant view of this character type, it is probably reflective of his own attitude toward conscious or unconscious feelings and fantasies of rebellion. It would be a rare reader who would consciously admit to any feelings of identification with the rogue; yet since this literary type has remained a charmer throughout the ages, it seems viable to consider him in terms of reader emotional response.

On first encounter, Panurge seems likeable albeit pathetic. Since he is hungry and thirsty, Pantagruel gives him some wine: "Mais le pauvre Panurge en beut vaillamment, car il estoit eximé comme un haran soret" (*Pantagruel*, 288). He tells the story of how the Turks have mistreated him: "Les Paillards Turcqs m'avoient mys en broche tout lardé comme un connil, car j'estois tant eximé que aultrement de ma chair eust esté

48. Heilman, p. 104.
49. Heilman, p. 105.·
50. Heilman, p. 106.

fort maulvaise viande; et en ce poinct me faisoyent roustir tout vif" (*Pantagruel,* 289). But he was clever enough to escape from an impossible situation. Having noticed that the "routisseur" has fallen asleep, Panurge says, "Lors je prens avecques les dents un tyson par le bout où il n'estoit point bruslé, et vous le gette au gyron de mon routisseur, et un aultre je gette, le mieulx que je peuz, soubz un lict de camp qui estoit auprès de la cheminée où estoit la paillasse de Monsieur mon routisseur. Incontinent le feu se print à la paille, et de la paille au lict, et du lict au solier, qui estoit embrunché de sapin faict à quehues de lampes" (*Pantagruel,* 289-90).

In the fifteenth chapter, although Panurge's humor is rather macabre, it is still funny and creative. When he remarks that the walls of Paris are poor defenses against an enemy, Pantagruel responds that the costs of an adequate wall would be monumental. Panurge answers proudly: "Je leurs enseigneray une maniere bien nouvelle comment ilz les pourront bastir à bon marché" (*Pantagruel,* 296). He describes his plan:

> Je voy que les callibistrys des femmes de ce pays sont à meilleur marché que les pierres. D'iceulx fauldroit bastir les murailles, en les arrengeant par bonne symmeterye d'architecture et mettant les plus grans au premiers rancz, et puis, en taluant à doz d'asne, arranger les moyens et finablement les petitz, puis faire un beau petit entrelardement, a poinctes de diamans comme la grosse tour de Bourges, de tant de bracquemars enroiddys qui habitent par les braguettes claustrales. (*Pantagruel,* 296)

However, in chapter xvi the portrait of Panurge changes; his humor is aggressive and his tricks sadistic. The reader is led away from the joyful, funloving Panurge of chapter xv who is described as "ayant tousjours le flacon soubz sa robbe et quelque morceau de jambon: car sans cela jamais ne alloit il, disant que c'estoit son garde-corps. Aultre espée ne portoit il, et, quand Pantagruel luy en voulut bailler une, il respondit qu'elle luy eschaufferoit la ratelle" (*Pantagruel,* 294). In chapter xvi Panurge has become someone who "portoit ordinairement un fouet soubz sa robbe, duquel il fouettoyt sans remission les paiges, qu'il trouvoit portans du vin à leurs maistres, pour les avancer d'aller" (*Pantagruel,* 302). In addition to the sword under his cloak, Panurge has twenty-six pockets in the cloak which are full of every kind of mischievous device. Some of the items are a knife, grape-juice, burrs, horns, lice, hooks and buckles, matches, needles, itching powder, oil, a picklock and so forth. In and of themselves these articles could be most useful, but this is not the reason Panurge has them. In one pocket

Panurge has "un petit cousteau, affilé comme l'aguille d'un peletier, dont il couppoit les bourses; l'autre, de aigrest, qu'il gettoit aux yeulx de ceulx qu'il trouvoit; l'aultre, de glaterons empenez de petites plumes de oysons ou de chappons, qu'il gettoit sus les robes et bonnetz des bonnes gens" (*Pantagruel*, 302-03). Whatever Panurge may not gain by charm or wit, he is prepared to take by devious force. The rogue "takes by trick what he could earn by effort; dazzles rather than seek respect."[51] In chapter xvi Panurge's sadistic humor is aimed against the guard, "le guet", against scholars, "maistres es ars", and according to some editions of Rabelais against the theologians. The tricks played against "le guet" are merely in humorous bad taste. First, Panurge persuades some yokels to drink too much in order to obtain their assistance. Then when the guard is coming up the hill, they push a dung-cart which knocks over the members of the guard (*Pantagruel*, 301). The other trick consists of setting fire to gunpowder just as the guard walks by (*Pantagruel*, 301-02). The first trick played against the scholars is again simply boisterous fun which is in bad taste. Panurge puts dung in their hoods (*Pantagruel*, 302). The second trick pulled on these men negates the portrait of Panurge as a poor, mistreated fellow who retaliates by practical jokes:

> Un jour que l'on avoit assigné à yceulx se trouver en la rue du Feurre, il feist une tartre Borbonnoise, composée de force de hailz, de "galbanum", de "assa foetida", de "castoreum", d'estroncs tous chaulx, et la destrampit en sanie de bosses chancreuses, et de fort bon matin engressa et oignit tout le pavé, en sorte que le diable n'y eust pas duré. Et tous ces bonnes gens rendoyent là leurs gorges devant tout le monde, comme s'ilz eussent escorché le renard: et en mourut dix ou douze de peste, quatorze en feurent ladres, dix et huyct, en furent pouacres, et plus de vingt et sept en eurent la verolle. Mais il ne s'en soucioit mie. (*Pantagruel*, 302)

From one perspective it might be said that Panurge's tricks are symbolic of Rabelais's attacks against the institutions of his time — the court, the university, the Church. In chapter xvii Panurge continues the same sort of behavior although it is within the context of his pretending to help others. It almost seems as if he realizes that he must hide his sadistic impulses or at least clothe them in terms of a surface generosity. He tells Pantagruel that at one time he possessed a fortune acquired from the Crusades. However, he has lost this fortune by giving it away to deserving people. He has arranged marriages and wedding feasts for the

---

51. Heilman, p. 104.

oldest and ugliest prostitutes (*Pantagruel,* 309-10). He gives banquets for the court pages (*Pantagruel,* 311). The reader may feel that Panurge's tricks really come from a basic desire to aid the victims of society's seemingly invincible authorities. From this standpoint the reader, depending on his personal feelings and fantasies, may think that Panurge's victims deserve what they get. Panurge may have stolen money from the Crusades and from the Church, but, after all, he is so poor and they are so rich. And, he certainly is kind to the pages for in addition to giving them banquets, he lays a complaint before the court to the effect that the mules of the high officials so spoil the pavement that the pages cannot play there (*Pantagruel,* 311). However, this Robin Hood portrait of Panurge is destroyed when he admits that one of his biggest laughs comes from knowing that the Masters sometimes blame their pages for some of his tricks and consequently beat them: "Mais je me rys encores dadvantage, c'est que, eulx arrivez au logis, ilz font fouetter monsieur du paige comme seigle vert. Par ainsi, je ne plains poinct ce que m'a cousté à les bancqueter" (*Pantagruel,* 312). The reader is forced to acknowledge that in spite of Panurge's apparent generosity, his sadistic traits are not eradicated. Heilman characterizes the rogue as one without real moral concern:

> Since in the life of "wits" certain functions of the mind dominate, this life also means a diminution, if not total elimination, of emotional depths and moral concern. The rogue is without conscience or superego or the inhibitions created by the community's sense of right and wrong.[52]

Yet the rogue is not entirely without feelings. He may feel fear, but rarely terror; he may be interested in sex "but he hardly experiences passion or serious jealousy, and least of all love."[53] Having used roguish tricks to defeat Thaumaste, Panurge believes himself to be invincible; thus he relies on his reputation and his boldness to try to win the sexual favors of a great lady of Paris:

> Panurge commença estre en reputation en la ville de Paris par ceste disputation que il obtint contre l'Angloys, et faisoit des lors bien valoir sa braguette . . . . Et le monde le louoit publicquement, et en feust faicte une chanson, dont les petitz enfans alloyent à la moustarde, et estoit bien venu en toutes compaignies de dames et demoiselles, en sorte qu'il devint glorieux, si bien qu'il entreprint venir au dessus d'une des grandes dames de la ville. (*Pantagruel,* 326)

When the lady rejects him, Panurge prepares a revenge worthy of the

---

52. Heilman, p. 102.
53. Heilman, p. 103.

character type called rogue: " 'Bren pour vous. Il ne vous appartient tant de bien ny de honneur; mais par Dieu, je vous feray chevaucher aux chiens.' Et ce dict, s'en fouit le grand pas, de peur des coups, lesquelz il craignoit naturellement" (*Pantagruel,* 331). A tension has been created between his grandiose feelings of rebellion and the insecure feelings created by rejection. If the rogue is rebuffed, although he still has no emotional depth, he may decide to play a role in which he seeks to experience real feelings, real acceptance. Panurge in *Pantagruel* is sexually rejected by the great lady and is scolded by Alcofrybas for his irresponsibility; thus the stage is set for the character traits of insecurity and uncertainty which are manifested in *Le Tiers Livre*. Like the rogue who assumes various identities, the child alternates among various roles in his quest for social acceptance, maturity and socialization. And at the level of emotional response, the reader can identify with the quest of the rogue and the child for acceptance; the reader who silently cheered the asocial behavior of the rogue is ready to repent of his fantasies of rebellion by identifying with complementary feelings and fantasies of punishment, loss, rejection and the insecurity implicit in these feelings.

Panurge's bag of tricks contains two kinds other than the aggressive, sadistic ones. In chapters xviii and xix, Panurge's tricks border on ludicrous silliness. The tricks played in chapters xxx and xxxi make use of magic. In chapter xviii, Thaumaste, a great English scholar, comes to France to debate with Pantagruel who also has a wide reputation for being wise and learned. However, says Thaumaste: "Je ne veulx disputer en la maniere des academicques par declamation, ny aussi par nombres, comme faisoit Pythagoras et comme voulut faire Picus Mirandula à Romme; mais je veulx disputer par signes seulement, sans parler, car les matieres sont tant ardues que les parolles humaines ne seroyent suffisantes à les expliquer à mon plaisir" (*Pantagruel,* 314). Pantagruel responds, "Nous confererons de tes doubtes ensemble, et en chercherons la resolution jusques au fond du puis inespuisable auquel disoit Heraclite estre la verité cachée" (315). On an intellectual level, Rabelais has thus prepared the reader to experience a deeply philosophical quest for truth. To enhance further this interpretation of the discussion which is in preparation, both scholars are thirsty the night before the debate; thirst is used throughout Rabelais's work as a symbol of the desire for acquisition of knowledge. When Pantagruel decides to permit Panurge, his "disciple", to replace him in the discussion, the reader wonders what will happen to the supposed serious matter. As could be expected,

Panurge turns the affair into a farce. By making ridiculous faces and bizarre noises, he wins the debate. On one level, this treatment of a "serious" quest for truth is a satire of the pretentious intellectuality of many scholars of the time. From another point of view, this farce is analogous to Rabelais's suggestion that the reader seek out the "sustantificque mouelle" of the bone; there is a hint of the idea that roguish, enigmatic Panurge may possess some truth which lies beyond rational, intellectual knowledge. Perhaps there are important truths that lie in the realm of emotional, irrational, uncivilized behavior.

Panurge's magic tricks symbolically express fantasies of grandeur. Like the aggressive tricks, these magic tricks are metaphors for the feeling or fantasy of having total control of one's world. In chapter xxx Epistemon is killed in battle. Panurge brings him back to life by sewing his head back onto his body. The magic trick performed in chapter xxxi of the *Pantagruel* is much less impressive. Placing a stick on top of two glasses filled with water and placed five feet apart, Panurge asks a friend to strike the stick in the middle with his spear. The friend does this without breaking the glasses or spilling the water.

Thus, in this chapter one has portrayed Panurge as a real character to whom the reader may relate emotionally insofar as he is the agent of expression for basic fantasies and feelings. It was argued in the first chapter that the life rhythm of the emotions is a complex of tensions wherein there is continually conflict/resolution. At the level of conflict one may feel aggressive, may wish to attack the source of his conflict; within this context Panurge is the rogue, manipulating his world through a series of attacks and rebellions. At the level of resolution, one may feel relief, superiority, exuberance; within this perspective Panurge is a stock-type, comic character, controlling his world through joyous, raucous fun. Seen in Rabelais's work as a whole, roguish Panurge is expressive of the two essential facets of the form, comedy and satire. Perhaps Rabelais through Panurge is suggesting a basic philosophy of the human condition: if one attacks the ills of the world and then laughs at them, maybe he will attain some sort of balance that will make his life more bearable.

CHAPTER III: PANURGE AS CHILD

This chapter will give a more detailed answer to the questions: Who is Panurge? What is his function in the whole of Rabelais's work? The critical viewpoint delineated in the first two chapters of this study suggests that the reader relates to and "re-creates" a work through his own emotions as well as through his intellect; the specific focus for "re-creation" is literary character. Although a cursory description has been offered as to how Panurge is illustrative of this critical position, a more exact study is necessary.

It is somewhat difficult to speak of emotional rhythm in Rabelais for the style is often uneven, the language sometimes dense and the characters relatively undeveloped. Nonetheless, there is a unifying force in Rabelais's work that binds together the disparate facets, making of it a classic work of literature. This study has labeled that cohesive element, the emotional current to which readers through the ages respond. In Rabelais, the essential expression of the emotional rhythm belongs to Panurge, of whom it has been said: "Voilà l'âme du livre."[1]

Susanne Langer's description of emotion was used in chapter I: "Feeling and emotion are really complexes of tension."[2] Many critics accept the idea that to varying degrees works of art, be they painting, architecture, music or literature, are made up of complexes of tensions, both in form and in content: in this context, literary character as bearer of emotional charge, and thereby implicitly of tension, becomes a microcosm of the work itself. Panurge depicts the irrational, irrepressible, rebellious spirit often attributed to Rabelais. Through the same "asocial" aspect of human nature, the reader creates a personal image of Panurge, filling in the picture with whatever fantasies, feelings and implicit tensions he may have about his own social self. For instance, an iconoclast may joyfully cheer Panurge's exploits while a proper lady,

---

1. Alfred Mayrargues, *Rabelais: Etude sur le seizième siècle* (Paris: Librairie Hachette et Cie, 1868), p. 129.
2. Susanne K. Langer, *Feeling and Form: A Theory of Art* (New York: Charles Scribner's Sons, 1953), p. 74.

carefully masked and repressed, may frown, unaware that it is a frown of recognition. One may well ask how universal appeal can be assigned to an asocial character, for many readers will readily take an oath that they have never been rebellious, mischievous or sadistic and certainly have no feelings or fantasies at all related to such behavior. Yet, a look at the physical development of the human species reveals that during childhood and adolescence there are certain tensions relatively common to all, partially because of the inherent physical states of those periods. The facts of physical smallness and emerging sense of identity tend to cause feelings of fear, anger and insecurity and consequent fantasies of rebellion and omnipotence. The psychologist Erik Erikson feels that, "Long childhood makes a technical and mental virtuoso out of man, but it also leaves a lifelong residue of emotional immaturity in him."[3] Through the residues of tension which remain in the adult because of the experiences, feelings and fantasies of his long childhood, the reader may recognize a part of himself in Panurge.

As one who does not fit harmoniously into adult society, into the structured framework of his milieu, Panurge has been variously interpreted as symbol of natural or primitive man, as a rogue, as a rebel, as a neurotic and as pure pretext for entertaining an adult audience. A configuration which represents all these character types is that of the child. Obviously, one cannot consider Panurge as a child from a physical point of view for he has the appearance and physical attributes of a man middle-aged in Rabelais's day. Too, he possesses the skill of language. Finally, he can support himself economically albeit his methods are not honest or productive. Thus, any description of Panurge as child refers only to his emotional being. Panurge is often stupid, a trickster, irrational while Pantagruel is intelligent, wise, reasonable, good and possesses common sense as well. Those characteristics attributed to Pantagruel could describe, on an ideal plane, a mature adult, while those given to Panurge could characterize a child (a neurotic, a madman or a primitive).

To discern what is child-like in Panurge, one must first consider the concept of maturity which ideally characterizes the state of adulthood. To risk a general definition of "maturity" is to reflect a drastic diversity of opinion. One conception characterizes the mature individual as one

---

3. Erik H. Erikson, *Childhood and Society* (New York: W. W. Norton and Company, Inc., 1963), p. 16.

who accepts the dictates of God, country and family and carries them out responsibly. In direct opposition, another concept views the mature person as one who questions the framework of traditional answers and tries to live wisely in light of his doubts. However, there is a description broad enough to allow for various kinds of mature development. Vexliard says: "Un point sur lequel tous les auteurs sont d'accord, c'est que la notion de maturité implique celle de l'indépendance, au sens psychologique."[4] Psychological independence is linked to the concept of freedom, defined in chapter II as that state in which one is relatively free to make his own choices and accept the consequent responsibilities for them. Vexliard continues, citing E. Mounier for confirmation:

> Un adulte complet est un être qui agit par soi, ce qui ne veut pas dire qu'il agisse et qu'il juge seul, mais il le fait en dernier ressort, ce dernier ressort lui dictât-il de se confier volontairement non par soutien ou par faiblesse, à un autre jugement, à une autre direction que les siens.[5]

Maturity in the Western world is achieved or not through the manner in which one deals with the coming-of-age crisis. In his book *What It Means to Grow Up,* Fritz Künkel says:

> To grow up, means to learn again from the ground up; it means learning essentially anew. Growing up, coming of age, implies a readiness to re-learn again and again, to change again and again and become still more mature. To be mature means to face, and not evade, every fresh crisis that comes.[6]

Out of the multitude of crises which involve family, peers and society at large, an individual develops an attitude toward the world, a philosophy of life. Panurge as prototypical child in crisis in *Le Tiers Livre* and *Le Quart Livre* is also appropriate symbol of the Renaissance era when many individuals were trying to make personal choices which might free them from the confines of traditional ideas and authorities.

Concepts of maturity date from ancient mythologies as well as from twentieth century psychological findings. Generally speaking, in mythologies there are three stages of life: old age which possesses the attribute of wisdom; adulthood which gives claim to responsibility;

4. Alexandre Vexliard, *Le Clochard: Etude de psychologie sociale* (Paris: Desclée de Brouwer, 1957), p. 85.
5. Vexliard, p. 250.
6. Fritz Künkel, *What it Means to Grow Up: A Guide to Understanding the Development of Character,* trans. Barbara Keppel-Compton and Hulda Niebuhr (New York: Charles Scribner's Sons, 1944), p. 180.

childhood which is characterized by dependency.[7] The stage of dependency is described in mythologies as lacking freedom. At this stage of life, a person needs a structured world, for his insufficiency of physical, intellectual and emotional development makes it difficult for him to tolerate too much tension or frustration. As long as he is in a relatively secure environment, however, a child may have the feeling that he is omnipotent, that there are no limitations of reality on him. The moment his security is removed and he thus loses control of his world, his feeling is one of impotence which may call forth various reactions of anger, aggression, fear, passivity. He has become powerless and must seek in some way to reaffirm his very existence. When Panurge is removed from the utopic security of the *Pantagruel,* he loses the illusion of freedom and omnipotence; in *Le Tiers Livre* and *Le Quart Livre* he faces the necessary crises of a child trying to grow up.

There have always been children in literature who have frequently fulfilled essentially technical functions. Jung calls attention to the child god who serves as mythical hero of a people.[8] Fiedler speaks of the kind of child character who represents insight, innocence, rebirth and thus serves to recall the forgotten, lost or imagined paradise of one's past.[9] Since Panurge is neither a mythical god nor an innocent, he provides a technical function often fulfilled by a third kind of literary child. This type of child is frequently introduced to maintain a difficult point of view; a sort of "peeping Tom", he affords the author a tool for satire, a way to criticize the adult world while making the criticism seem innocuous.[10] Through Panurge's antics, rebelliousness and questioning, Rabelais satirizes certain individuals and institutions of his day; moreover, he satirizes the basic structure of society itself and ultimately, traditionally accepted metaphysical concepts regarding what is natural.

The idea of the child comes into play in Rabelais's books in three important ways. First, the concrete fact of childhood is dealt with in the presentation of the physical births and childhoods of Gargantua and

7. Joseph Campbell, "Man and Myth", *Psychology Today,* 5, No. 2 (July, 1971), 35-39 and 86-95.

8. Carl G. Jung and C. Kerényi, *Essays on a Science of Mythology: The Myths of the Divine Child and the Divine Maiden,* trans., R. F. C. Hull (New York: Harper and Row, 1949), pp. 84-85.

9. Leslie A. Fiedler, *No! in Thunder* (Boston: Beacon Press, 1960), p. 252.

10. Fiedler, p. 280.

of Pantagruel and is extended in descriptions of the formal education of the two giants. Secondly, the theme of immortality gained through one's children runs throughout Rabelais's work. Finally, some of the fantasies and feelings of the emotional aspect of childhood are illustrated through Panurge; this interpretation, a purely symbolic one, is the basis for the mimetic view of Panurge in terms of reader "re-creation".

The birth and education of Pantagruel are briefly recounted in *Pantagruel*. In the second chapter one learns that because of his monstrous size, Pantagruel's mother died when he was born. Chapter iv recounts the marvelous feats of physical strength performed while he was yet a baby. For example, at each meal Pantagruel drank the milk of four thousand six hundred cows.[11] In chapter v one finds that he went to Poitiers to study and did very well. At Toulouse he learned to dance and use a sword. Later, at Montpellier he considered studying medicine but decided against it, choosing rather to study law at Bourges. His education ends at Orléans where he learns to play tennis. Actually one knows little about Pantagruel's youth except that he was physically strong and relatively well educated. From this scanty information, one might conclude that childhood as a formative period for Pantagruel has little importance. Michel Beaujour observes:

> L'enfance dans *Pantagruel*, n'est qu'un motif imposé, prétexte à merveilleux, présage des exploits à venir, mais ne présente aucun intérêt intrinsèque. Il ne s'agit pas de décrire un enfant, mais un héros qui se dissimule encore sous l'apparence du nourrisson. Cette enfance n'est qu'un masque diaphane, et une source de contrastes propres à provoquer le rire et à manifester la quasi divinité du héros . . . . Le héros mythique n'est jamais enfant qu'en apparence.[12]

If one can attribute any symbolic meaning to Pantagruel's childhood, it seems to come from its animality. Because of the influence of twentieth century psychological findings, it is now a generally accepted idea that babies are physical creatures centering much of their existence on bodily needs and functions. In his description of Pantagruel's infancy, Rabelais has magnified an ordinary baby's physical nature thousands of time, possibly suggesting that the reader direct his attention to physical nature itself. Certainly a major theme in *Pantagruel, Gargantua* and *Le Tiers Livre* is the goodness and naturalness of man's sensuous side. The

---

11. Rabelais, *Pantagruel, Oeuvres complètes*, vol. I, ed., Pierre Jourda (Paris: Editions Garnier Frères, 1962), p. 235.
12. Michel Beaujour, *Le Jeu de Rabelais* (Issoudun: Editions de l'Herne, 1969), p. 67.

treatment of the concept of "natural" in regard to man's physical nature leads logically to various passages which consider just what natural means in law, religion and customs. In *Le Quart Livre* Rabelais conducts a much more extensive examination of the concept of "natural" than in the preceding three books.

As Pantagruel grows into a young man, his physical dimensions appear to be human. Only when he engages in war does his gigantism reappear. This suggests that in *Pantagruel* gigantism is metaphorically important in describing man's physical nature: Pantagruel is a giant when he consumes large quantities of food and when he proves his physical superiority through military conquest. *Gargantua,* which appeared two years later, adds to the list of gigantic feats that of learning.[13]

In *Gargantua* both the childhood and education of this giant are dwelt on at length. That Gargantua is going to be a miracle child is indicated by the strange nature of his birth; he was carried for eleven months and finally entered the world through his mother's left ear. To confirm this uniqueness, he is able to use language from the moment he is born; on arrival he cries, "A boire! à boire! à boire! "[14] The giant baby's bodily functions are those of any normal child, except that they are amplified beyond comprehension. He sleeps, drinks and eats enormous amounts and "se conchioit à toutes heures" (*Gargantua,* 34). In every aspect of his life he is a physical creature:

> Tousjours se vaultroit par les fanges, se mascaroyt le nez, se chauffourroit le visaige, aculoyt ses souliers, baisloit souvent au mousches, et couroit voulentiers après les parpaillons, desquelz son pere tenoit l'empire. Il pissoit sus ses souliers, il chyoit en sa chemise, il se mouschoyt à ses manches, il mourvoit dedans sa souppe, et patroilloit par tout lieux, et beuvoit . . . . Ses dens aguysoit d'un sabot, ses mains lavoit de potaige, se pignoit d'un goubelet, se asseoyt entre deux selles le cul à terre, se couvroyt d'un sac mouillé, . . . mordoyt en riant, rioyt en mordent, souvent crachoyt on bassin, pettoyt de gresse, pissoyt contre le soleil . . . . Les petitz chiens de son pere mangeoient en son escuelle: luy de mesmes mangeoit avecques eux. Il leurs mordoit les aureilles, ilz luy graphinoient le nez; il leurs souffloit au cul, ilz luy leschoient les badigoinces. (*Gargantua,* 48-9)

Thus, the joy which Gargantua finds in his animal nature is lyrically

---

13. Beaujour notes that, "Dans *Gargantua*, les différences tiennent moins à la taille et à la force physique qu'à l'agilité mentale, et au savoir." Beaujour, p. 68.

14. Rabelais, *Gargantua, Oeuvres complètes*, vol. I, ed., Pierre Jourda (Paris: Editions Garnier Frères, 1962), p. 31.

painted; he frolics with the butterflies and eats from the same dish as his father's dogs. Bodily delights do not stop with playing, eating, sleeping and toilet functions. Still a baby, Gargantua sexually titillates his governesses and is sexually stimulated by them. The sensual delight of the little giant's childhood becomes symbolic of a natural spontaneity and freedom possible only in childhood. In the opinion of Michel Beaujour:

> Identifiée à la nature – au plaisir et à l'animalité – l'enfance l'est aussi à la folie: même liberté face au sens commun, à la hiérarchie, à l'opposition sacro-sainte du haut et du bas. Ce monde à l'envers, ce chaos de la non distinction, c'est aussi le carnaval .... L'enfance, au sein d'une culture donnée, est le plus long carnaval. En effet, l'accumulation des proverbes parvient à généraliser la condition de cet enfant-là: ce n'est plus le petit Gargantua, mais l'Enfance (et peut-être aussi, par analogie, la nature, l'animalité, la folie), qui s'oppose ici au Sérieux, et triomphe fugacement grâce à la poésie.15

With a sudden break, Gargantua's total way of life is changed; symbolically cast from the Garden of Eden, his idle, animal existence is ended. Ponocrates, his tutor, has decided that he needs a more serious kind of education. Antithetic to his former way of life, the new regime beginning at 4:00 A.M. calls for a martial, puritanic discipline. Study of the sciences, philosophy, literature, the Bible and the arts, as well as playing games and sports which demand dexterity and physical strength, make up his daily schedule. The world of the natural child, where physical freedom and spontaneity set the tone is replaced by an artificial "boarding school" atmosphere where mind and body must be rigorously trained. Symbolically primitive man has evolved to social man.

Despite the fact that Gargantua's educational program is gigantic, there is still a reduction to the human level. While the reader will never be able to view the world from the dizzy heights of the giant's superhuman feats, he can identify with the potential for superhuman efforts expended to develop the mind. Subtly, gradually, Rabelais has drawn the reader into the world of his work, leading him away from the fabulous realm of the impossible to an abstract, yet seemingly possible idea of gianthood. Fittingly, Pantagruel and Gargantua have evolved away from the poet's vision of childhood into respectable adults, dedicated to ruling their subjects kindly and wisely. By this very process, says Freud, civilizations are built by man's sublimating the energies of

15. Beaujour, p. 72.

his childhood animal nature into the service of a larger community.[16] On the other hand, Panurge's continual obsession with his carnal nature makes him an example of unrepressed, unsocialized man and thus he presents a perpetual image of childhood spontaneity.

A second instance of Rabelais's focus on the period of childhood is his preoccupation with genealogies and with the theme of immortality gained through one's children. It has been frequently noted that Rabelais's books parody medieval epics. In the thirteenth and fourteenth centuries, French *trouvères* attached then current *chansons de geste* to the earlier *chansons,* dating from the eleventh century, in order to group the poems into cycles which recounted the adventures of a particular hero and of his ancestors, friends and children.[17] In trying to correctly group these epic poems into the appropriate cycles the *trouvères* were preoccupied with the question of lineage, a preoccupation which Rabelais's genealogies parody. Rabelais may also have parodied Biblical concern with lineage. In any case, Rabelais is clearly making fun of the passion for identifying oneself with one's ancestry. Perhaps he is suggesting that the "material" (external) concern with who begat whom is not as important as a "spiritual" (internal) emphasis on situating oneself in a different kind of tradition, giving oneself a uniquely individual childhood; thus Pantagruel and Gargantua follow an unorthodox path in their quest for intellectual growth and Panurge follows a highly personal route in his search for emotional growth.

Secondly, Rabelais's use of genealogy serves the technical function of disorienting the reader, whetting his curiosity as to how serious the work is, for the genealogies pretend to situate the books in a serious tradition. By extension, Renaissance man sought to place himself within a civilized tradition, to give the childhood of his rebirth a history.

Chapter i of *Gargantua* refers the reader to the first chapter of *Pantagruel:*

> Je vous remectz à la grande chronicque Pantagrueline recongnoistre la genealogie et antiquité dont nous est venu Gargantua. En icelle vous entendrez plus au long comment les geands nasquirent en ce monde, et comment d'iceulx, par lignes directes, yssit Gargantua, père de Pantagruel, et ne vous faschera si pour le present je m'en deporte, combien que la chose soit telle que, tant plus seroit remembrée, tant plus elle plairoit à vos Seigneuries. (*Gargantua,* 11)

16. J. A. C. Brown, *Freud and the Post-Freudians* (Baltimore: Penguin Books, 1967), pp. 116-17.

17. André Lagarde and Laurent Michard, *Moyen Age: Les Grands Auteurs français du programme* (Bordas: Collection Textes et Littérature, 1962), p. 2.

This genealogy fills the first chapter of *Pantagruel,* logically preceding the chapters on Pantagruel's birth, education and youth. The subject of immortality gained through one's children immediately follows in chapter viii. In a letter to Pantagruel, Gargantua says:

> Entre les dons, graces et prerogatives desquelles le souverain plasmateur Dieu tout puissant à endouayré et aorné l'humaine nature à son commencement, celle me semble singuliere et excellente par laquelle elle peut, en estat mortel, acquerir une espece de immortalité, et, en decours de vie transitoire, perpetuer son nom et sa semence. Ce que est faict par lignée yssue de nous en mariage legitime. (*Pantagruel,* 256)

The thread of this theme is carried into *Le Tiers Livre*; one of the reasons given by Panurge for his desire to marry is that he wants a legitimate son to carry on his name. His statement of this wish comes about indirectly. Panurge asks Pantagruel why newly married men are exempt from war during the first year of their marriage:

> Scelon mon jugement (respondit Pantagruel) c'estoit affin que pour la premiere année, ilz jouissent de leurs amours à plaisir, vacassent à production de lignage et feissent provision de heritiers; ainsi pour le moins, si l'année seconde estoient en guerre occis, leur nom et armes restast en leurs enfans.[18]

In chapter vii Panurge announces his decision to marry, although he soon after begins to manifest doubts about this decision. Pantagruel, disturbed at his friend's uncertainty, advises him not to marry, to which Panurge replies: "Voire mais . . . je n'aurois jamais aultrement filz ne filles legitimes, es quelz j'eusse espoir mon nom et armes perpetuer, es quelz je puisse laisser mes heritaiges et acquestz" (*Le Tiers Livre,* 440).

Perhaps Rabelais, aging, unmarried, without a legitimate son, at odds with the society of his time, seeks through writing both to find and to affirm himself and thereby to create for himself a symbolic immortality. Rollo May speaks for a mimetic interpretation of the writing process:

> No writer writes out of his having found the answer to the problem; he writes rather out of his having the problem and "wanting" a solution. The solution consists not of a resolution. It consists of the "deeper and wider dimension of consciousness to which the writer is carried by virtue of his wrestling with the problem."[19]

---

18. Rabelais, *Le Tiers Livre, Oeuvres complètes,* vol. I, ed., Pierre Jourda (Paris: Editions Garnier Frères, 1962), pp. 427-28.

19. Rollo May, *Love and Will* (New York: W. W. Norton and Company, Inc., 1969), pp. 170-71.

Rabelais's preoccupation with the legitimacy of one's children may reflect his desire that the work be seen as authentic despite its many borrowings and almost direct imitations. And the authentic aspect, the part that is most subjectively Rabelais, is perhaps the emotional quest for strength, development and understanding. Panurge as emotional child portrays the conflict; his quest becomes synonymous with the abstract idea of searching. The work is the resolution – the legitimate claim to immortality.

Question/response, conflict/resolution are raised to the plane of language where they merge in the verbalization of their paradoxical co-existence. And as the words go together to make up the total work, the artist symbolically gives birth to a kind of child. At the same time the artist himself resembles a child, charming, tricking, controlling and always omnipotent in the secure world of the work. The reader enters a work in an emotional pact with the author, a pact wherein he feels and fantasizes his own conflicts and resolutions through the veil of words. Because the feelings and fantasies are controlled for him by the work itself, he may allow his own inner life a free rein withheld in daily living. In this sense, the reader, too, is a sort of child, paradoxically all powerful because of the fact that he is in a secure realm. Finally, much like the yet asocial child who represents the antithesis of the repressions of civilization, the artist undoes the repressions of society and invites the reader to participate in that experience:

> The artist is the man who refuses initiation through education into the existing order, remains faithful to his own childhood being, and thus becomes "a human being in the spirit of all times, an artist."[20]

Within this context, Panurge's quest for a meaningful existence both within society and outside its restrictions, is Rabelais's quest. Panurge's symbolic childhood becomes the artist's quest for vision and salvation.

The giants pass rapidly from the animal side of childhood to the age of reason. Rigid, formal education prepares them to become model rulers in their society. The something lacking in their development as human beings is supplied by Panurge who as emotional being bridges the gap between the animal aspect of man's nature and his rational, intellectual side. In *Pantagruel* Panurge is happy and carefree. The world seems open to receive him. The beautiful childhood dream is destroyed in *Le Tiers Livre* when Pantagruel pays Panurge's debts and

20. J. A. C. Brown, p. 67.

demands that he become a responsible adult. In the throes of trying to become civilized, Panurge will learn that there are limitations on his power, although, typical of the child, he fights to retain control of a world in which he is central, a world in which he is unaware of others except insofar as they enhance him. One of the major facets of Panurge's child-likeness in *Pantagruel* is his attempt to control and influence his world by indirect means such as playing tricks; a child, small in size and limited in repertoire of behavior often relies on tricks to win attention. Morton cites Freud's theory: "The child wants power and gets it as he can. . . . By self-display he creates a sensation and gets attention."[21] Charming is not a word that can be applied to Panurge's tricks, for most of them are at the least annoying and at the worst destructive. They run the gamut from throwing itching powder down the backs of vain women to tricking a sheep merchant into drowning (in *Le Quart Livre*). This last ploy bespeaks another potential characteristic of the child. Once more, it is useful to look to Freudian theory, as cited by Morton:

> Cruelty is especially near the childish character, since the inhibition which restrains the impulse to mastery before it causes pain to others, that is the capacity for sympathy, develops late.[22]

Panurge's dimensions, however, transcend those of the unfeeling rogue who remains rather consistently a trickster, for this is only one of the methods which he uses to assert himself. Other manifestations of his child-likeness are his spontaneous joy, his portrayal of the goodness and naturalness of one's physical nature through a lack of sexual inhibition and finally his direct apprehension of truth which is an ability attributed to children because they have not yet learned the repressions and hypocrisies of socialized man.

In *Pantagruel* Panurge gains in stature as he succeeds in duping so many pretentious members of society. Theologians, scholars, snobbish women are left unmasked and somewhat ridiculous. Once he aided a friar about to say mass to dress himself; for devilment Panurge sewed his alb onto his gown and shirt. When the unsuspecting priest, after saying mass before the gentlemen of the court, removed his alb, his gown and shirt came off as well, leaving them no recourse but to ask:

21. G. F. Morton, *Childhood's Fears: Psycho-Analysis and the Inferiority-Fear Complex* (New York: Macmillan Company, 1925), p. 145.
22. Morton, p. 142.

"Et quoy, ce beau pere nous veult icy faire l'offrande et baiser son cul? " (*Pantagruel*, 304). Another of Panurge's favorite tricks was to approach a man or woman dressed in finery and to compliment him or her, stroking the material while smearing nasty, staining oil on it (*Pantagruel*, 305). Nonetheless, minor practical jokes such as these did not prove Panurge to be the brave fellow he claimed to be. So, in chapter xxiii he sets about proving his true grandeur. Pantagruel's jolly band has just set out to defeat the Dipsodes who had invaded the country of the Amaurots. When Pantagruel's men arrived in the harbour, they saw six hundred and sixty knights coming toward them. Knowing his own strength and fearful for his friends, Pantagruel instructed his companions to return to the ship while he annihilated the interlopers. When cocky, little Panurge refuses, saying that Pantagruel must retire while he handles the situation, one is tempted to laugh. Playing practical jokes with pins, buckles, itching powder and face-making is not of the same order as defeating hundreds of soldiers. Yet, to one's surprise, Panurge refuses to be outdone by physical limitations; he transcends this handicap and defeats the knights by playing a clever trick. He takes two huge cables from the ship and ties them to the capstan on the deck. Then, he makes two large loops, putting one inside the other. To complete the basic plan, he spreads straw and gunpowder outside the circle of the cables. Two of Pantagruel's companions, then, pretend to surrender, thus attracting the knights on horseback into the circle of ropes. At this moment Epistemon turns the capstan, thus tripping the horses and dislodging the riders. And, with a final flourish, Panurge sets fire to the gunpowder, destroying all the men except one who is immediately captured and taken aboard (*Pantagruel*, 342-45).

Of course, the reader does not believe this exaggerated story. Nonetheless, at the feeling level of reader "re-creation", one can relate to the childhood fantasy of grandeur and glory. And the reader may smile, somehow reassured that the uneducated, the weak, the child, or possibly even himself, might use cleverness to attain difficult goals.

Unfortunately, most of Panurge's tricks do not come from altruistic motives. Even killing the enemy soldiers was not done just to save his companions, for Pantagruel could easily have done this; rather, childlike Panurge seized the opportunity to show off on a grand scale. The Panurge of chapter xxi, having just beaten Thaumuste in debate, is like a proud yet vain child who has just been voted the most popular boy in his class and believes that this gives him automatic permission to do anything he wishes. Decked in new finery: "Il devint glorieux, si bien

qu'il entreprint venir au dessus d'une des grandes dames de la ville"
(*Pantagruel*, 326). When the beautiful lady refuses Panurge's proffered
love, he, like a thwarted child, decides to take revenge, warning her of
his intent:

> Vous ne voulez doncques aultrement me laisser un peu faire? Bren pour vous. Il
> ne vous appartient tant de bien ny de honneur; mais par Dieu, je vous feray
> chevaucher aux chiens. (*Pantagruel*, 331)

To make good his threat, he sought her out the next day at a great feast
and sprinkled a powder on her dress which had the effect of attracting
hundreds of dogs and causing them to urinate on her. While the reader
may be both amused and disgusted by this childish reaction to rejection, he may have ever so slight a feeling of secret satisfaction. Although as an adult he may have learned to accept defeat as gracefully as
possible, could not he harbor some fantasy of revenge toward those
who have been involved in his own failures, no matter how minor?
Since, however, fiction is "untrue" and thus safe, the reader can assure
himself that only a neurotic, a savage, a madman or a child would
actually carry out so pure a retaliation.

Still, most of Panurge's tricks are played neither solely for the sake
of showing off nor for revenge, but simply to furnish him an occasion
to laugh at the expense of someone else. In chapter xvii he tells how he
cut the stirrups on the mules of the counselors so that when they tried
to mount, they fell flat on their faces. His egotistical lack of concern for
the feelings of others becomes clearer when he says that he played this
trick while the counselors' pages were feasting at a banquet that he
himself provided: "Mais je me rys encores dadvantage, c'est que, eulx
[les Conseilliers] arrivez au logis, ilz font fouetter monsieur du paige
comme seigle vert. Par ainsi, je ne plains poinct ce que m'a cousté à les
bancqueter" (*Pantagruel*, 312).

Although the Panurge of *Pantagruel* brags loudly about his sadistic
tricks, he intersperses this negative behavior with jollity, drinking and
feasting and thus is an adored child. Everybody looks at him, listens to
him and laughs at and with him. Like a child for whom any success is
possible, Panurge tells how he escaped from the Turks in face of impossible odds. Still reflecting unlimited confidence in himself, Panurge, in
chapter xix, confronts the famous English scholar Thaumaste, in debate. By making faces and obscene gestures, as do children at play,
Panurge confuses and charms his opponent and thus wins the debate.
After this victory, Panurge has not only the favor of Pantagruel and his
companions:

Panurge commença estre en reputation en la ville de Paris. . . . Et le monde le louoit publicquement, et en feust faicte une chanson, dont les petitz enfans alloyent à la moustarde, et estoit bien venu en toutes compaignies de dames et demoiselles, en sorte qu'il devint glorieux. (*Pantagruel*, 326)

His joy and boundless faith in self and the world is shown again in chapter xxix where he amuses three hundred enemy giants while Pantagruel, a little distance away, battles their captain:

Adonc se retirerent tous les geans avecques leur roy là auprès, où estoient les flaccons, et Panurge et ses compaignons avecques eulx, qui contrefaisoit ceulx qui ont eu la verolle, car il tordoit le gueulle et retiroit les doigtz; et, en parolle enrouée, leur dist: "Je renie bieu, compaignons, nous ne faisons poinct la guerre. Donnez nous à repaistre avecques vous, ce pendent que nos maistres s'entrebatent." A quoy voluntiers le roy et les geans consentirent, et les firent bancqueter avecques eulx. Ce pendent Panurge leur contoit les fables de Turpin, les exemples de saint Nicolas, et le conte de la Ciguoingne. (*Pantagruel*, 360)

Panurge, like a totally unencumbered child, free in his security, expresses direct responses of feeling, either through unsophisticated destruction or unmigitated joy. Scenes of joviality and sadism alternate, thus perpetuating the conflict/resolution rhythm of emotional configuration and thus maintaining the reader's emotional interest in the character.

Sexually uninhibited, Panurge acts as a prototype of natural, physical child. However, his concern with sexuality seems to remain at the verbal level, for his actions are not consistent with his boasts. One can delineate two clear-cut attitudes: glorification of his male sex organ and disdain for women, who are seen as unvirtuous creatures. The first attitude, his preoccupation with his supposed virility and potency, seems to be central to Panurge's image of himself throughout the works where he appears. When he feels omnipotent in his world, when his egotism is full-blown, he speaks of himself as a sexual giant. His first comment about his sex organ, albeit negative, is a boast about its dimensions. Having saved himself from being roasted by the Turks, he says: "Une jeune Corinthiace . . . regardoit mon pauvre haire esmoucheté comment il s'estoit retiré au feu, car il ne me alloit plus que jusques sur les genoulx" (*Pantagruel*, 293). In the same vein, when Pantagruel decides to dress Panurge in a manner befitting a cherished companion or child, Panurge's major concern is that his codpiece be magnificent:

– Vrayment, dist Pantagruel, tu es gentil compaignon, je te veulx habiller de ma livrée. – Et le feist vestir galantement selon la mode du temps qui couroit, excepté que Panurge voulut que la braguette de ses chausses feust longue de troys piedz et quarrée, non ronde, ce que feust faict; et la faisoit bon veoir. Et disoit souvent que le monde n'avoit encores congneu l'emolument et utilité qui est de porter grande braguette. (*Pantagruel*, 299-300)

In chapters xviii and xix the codpiece attains an importance beyond mere decoration. As Panurge prepares to debate the renowned Thaumaste, he prepares himself only by adding further ornamentation to his codpiece: "Or notez que Panurge avoit mis au bout de sa longue braguette un beau floc de soye rouge, blanche, verte et bleue, et dedans, avoit mis une belle pomme d'orange" (*Pantagruel*, 319). In Rabelais's time codpieces sometimes served as pockets (*Pantagruel*, footnote no.1, 319). And pockets have functioned traditionally to contain things or to hide something from view. In this light, one might view the codpiece symbolically; like a pocket, it hides from view the secret of man's naturalness, the secret of his vitality. This is not to suggest that Panurge wanted to hide the part which occasions so many boasts. Perhaps, again on a symbolic level, there is the indication that Panurge himself hides some important truth that one must delve below the surface to find. In this sense, the magnificent codpiece is a symbol of Panurge.

From another perspective the brightly colored codpiece becomes symbolic of Panurge's egotism; a show-off, an unsocialized child, he uses any means to draw attention to himself. In the nineteenth chapter the codpiece helps him win his debate:

> Panurge . . . tyra en l'air sa trèsmegiste braguette de la gausche, et de la dextre en tira un transon de couste bovine blanche et deux pieces de boys de forme pareille, l'une de ebene noir, l'aultre de bresil incarnat, et les mist entre les doigtz d'ycelle en bonne symmetrie, et, les chocquant ensemble, faisoyt son tel que font les ladres en Bretaigne avecques leurs clicquettes. (*Pantagruel*, 320)

Panurge's gestures and the brilliant colors distract the scholar who must yield to the trickster's clever ploy. Toward the end of the debate Panurge again uses his codpiece in a kind of lyric sexual boast:

> A quoy Panurge tira sa longue braguette avecques son floc, et l'estendit d'une couldée et demie, et la tenoit en l'air de la main gauche, et de la dextre print sa pomme d'orange, et, la gettant en l'air par sept foys, à la huytiesme la cacha au poing de la dextre, la tenant en hault tout coy; puis commença secouer sa belle braguette, la monstrant à Thaumaste. (*Pantagruel*, 322)

The codpiece has become analogous to the gown with twenty-six pockets, full of the various tricks which he uses to control the people in his world.

This chapter recounting the famous debate, where the pretext is a quest for hidden depths of truth, shows man in an irrational state, even silly and child-like. Yet if one is going to take Rabelais at all seriously, one must look beyond the farcical elements. There may be the suggestion that if there is some profound truth about man to be found, it lies beyond the realm of scholastic philosophy, even beyond the wisdom of the Ancients and abides in the domain of childlike spontaneity and naturalness. Fittingly, Panurge as victor is playful, uncivilized and ultimately sensual. In the next chapter Thaumaste says that Panurge has taught him new things about knowledge. Given the nature of the debate, it is certain that this learned scholar cannot be referring to verbalized theories about truth such as those expressed in philosophical or theological systems:

> Vous avez veu comment son seul disciple me a contenté en m'en a plus dict que n'en demandoys; d'abundand m'a ouvert et ensemble solu d'aultres doubtes inestimables. En quoy je vous puisse asseurer qu'il m'a ouvert le vrays puys et abisme de encyclopedie, voire en une sorte que je ne pensoys trouver homme qui en sceust les premiers elemens seulement. (*Pantagruel*, 325)

Due to the fame won in this debate, "Panurge commença estre en reputation en la ville de Paris . . . et faisoit des lors bien valoir sa braguette, et la feist au dessus esmoucheter de broderie à la Romanicque" (*Pantagruel*, 326). As Panurge's tricks and charm win for him a secure realm where he is loved and lauded, his symbolic ego, the sex organ, is changed from the poor, burnt member of chapter xiv to the gloriously arrayed phallus of chapter xxi. By the end of *Pantagruel* Panurge is so sure of himself and of his powers that he assures Pantagruel that he can defeat their enemy, the Dipsodes: "Merde, merde, (dist Panurge). Ma seulle braguette espoussetera tous les hommes" (*Pantagruel*, 349). Panurge has evolved to a symbolic gianthood.

In *Le Tiers Livre* Panurge's behavior is markedly different from that in *Pantagruel*; not only is he flawed, but also fallible. The confident braggart has become uncertain, insecure. One manifestation of this character change can be seen in his attitude towards his sexuality. Chapter vii tells of Panurge's shedding his magnificent codpiece, explaining that since he has decided to marry and will consequently be exempt from war for a year, he has no need of it, "car la braguette est premiere piece de harnoys pour armer l'homme de guerre" (*Le Tiers Livre*, 433). Yet removing the codpiece has meaning beyond the pragmatic reason that he will not need it as armor. His decision to marry means merging into the socialized, adult world. Thus, he sheds the symbol of his uniqueness, the sign of his remarkable prowess. Panurge is made sad by his decision; jewels are turned into sack-cloth, the childhood paradise has become the stark reality of the adult world. And, Panurge feels that by marrying, paying his debts and becoming socially responsible, he will be changing a personality which he wants to keep: "Puys qu'une foys je suis quitte, vous ne veistes oncques homme plus mal plaisant que je seray, si Dieu ne me ayde" (*Le Tiers Livre,* 431).

Since the Panurge of *Pantagruel* talked incessantly about all the women he had bedded, one might expect that he has decided to marry in order to be assured of a constantly available sexual partner. For the most part, however, his concerns are to find someone to care for him, to give him children and thus immortality, as well as to find someone who is virtuous and chaste and who will not beat, rob or cuckold him. Actually, there are only two instances in this book of the sexual braggadocio which was displayed throughout *Pantagruel,* both instances occasioned when Frère Jan suggests that Panurge might not be the sexual giant he claims. In chapter xxvii, the rowdy priest advises Panurge to marry in order to give himself the opportunity for continuous sexual exercise lest he lose his potency. Panurge fires back this response: "Je ne ignore que Salomon dict, et en parloit comme clerc et sçavant. Depuys luy Aristoteles a declairé l'estre des femmes estre de soy insatiable; mais je veulx qu'on saiche que, de mesmes qualibre, j'ay le ferrement infatiguable" (*Le Tiers Livre,* 518). Frère Jan continues to chide his friend to marry, using the argumentative ploy that as Panurge grows older he will totally lose his potency and must thus hurry to profit while he still may. Panurge's defensive reply is so exaggerated that one again sees his omnipotence as existing only in fantasy, only when he is not put to the test of reality: "Je te prie croyre (et ne croyras chose que ne soit vraye) mon naturel, le sacre Ithyphalle, messer Cotal d'Albingues, estre le *prime del monde*" (*Le Tiers Livre,* 518). To illustrate his point, he tells a story of being at a passion play where everyone, man and woman alike, desired him sexually, so mysteriously powerful was his animal appeal.

Freudian theory has provided the generally accepted knowledge that a child is not the asexual creature he was once thought to be. Rather, the very nature of childhood expresses itself through a concrete interpretation of the world, through the physical contact of touching, tasting, feeling. Thus, the child is a natural sensual being who enjoys displaying and touching his body. As he grows to adulthood, Western civilization teaches the child to hide both his body and his joy in it. Whether Panurge's sexual boasts have any basis in reality is unimportant, for as self-proclaimed sensual being, he symbolizes the uninhibited child who has been properly repressed in civilized man. Subliminal feelings and fantasies from childhood permit the individual reader to condemn or rejoice in Panurge's sexual giantism in *Pantagruel.* In *Le*

Tiers Livre and *Le Quart Livre* Panurge has evolved to child in crisis, to adolescence. Conscious of his body, yet unsure of what to do with his sexual feelings and fantasies, the "civilized" adolescent is appropriately insecure and frequently defensive. Doubt and confusion about his identity render the previously omnipotent child capable of striking out in anger at the hostile world which has usurped his supreme position. Within this context, one is not surprised when Panurge in *Le Quart Livre,* angered at Dindenault's insults about his sexual powers, ends by killing his taunter. The reader can relate to the fantasy of eradicating those who make him feel weak, small and ineffectual.

Panurge's second attitude in the sexual domain is one of disdain for women; they serve no function other than that of sex object. In *Pantagruel,* he refers to women as virtueless creatures, easily conquered by his overwhelming sexual power. And since women are so readily come by, Panurge even suggests their genitals as a cheap, available commodity for rebuilding the walls of Paris. After he finishes describing the manner in which this could be done, Pantagruel questions him: "Comment scez tu que les membres honteux des femmes sont à si bon marché, car en ceste ville il y a force preudes femmes, chastes et pucelles" (*Pantagruel,* 299). Panurge's answer is both a personal boast and an attack on female chastity:

> *Et ubi prenus*? dist Panurge. Je vous en diray, non oppinion, mais vraye certitude et asseurance. Je ne me vante d'en avoir embourré quatre cens dix et sept despuis que suis en ceste ville, — et n'y a que neuf jours, — mais, à ce matin, j'ay trouvé un bon homme qui, en un bissac tel comme celluy de Esopet portoit deux petites fillettes de l'eage de deux ou troys ans au plus, l'une davant, l'aultre derrière. Il me demande l'aulmosne, mais je luy feis responce que j'avoys beaucoup plus de couillons que de deniers, et après luy demande: "Bon homme, ces deux fillettes sont elles pucelles? " — Frere, dist il, il y a deux ans que ainsi je les porte, et, au regard de ceste cy devant, laquelle je voy continuellement, en mon advis elle est pucelle; toutesfoys, je n'en vouldroys mettre mon doigt au feu. Quand est de celle que je porte derriere, je ne sçay sans faulte rien. (*Pantagruel,* 299)

When the prisoner of the Dipsodes describes to Pantagruel and his men the army they will be opposing, he says that among the warriors and giants there are one hundred and fifty thousand whores. Not at all worried about defeating the thousands of soldiers, Panurge says that he is concerned about one thing: "C'est (dist Panurge), comment je pourray avanger à braquemarder toutes les putains qui y sont en ceste après disnée, qu'il n'en eschappe pas une que je ne taboure en forme commune" (*Pantagruel,* 348). In *Le Tiers Livre* women are still viewed as sexually insatiable creatures, not to be trusted, but Panurge's focus is different; while his attitude is a cause for the personal vanity of conquest in *Pantagruel,* it is a source of fear and insecurity in *Le Tiers Livre.* If women are not to be trusted, then, probably the one he chooses as a wife will betray him; he cannot endure the thought of losing face in such a manner. In *Pantagruel,* as long as Panurge was unencumbered by adult responsibility, he felt free to enjoy, or at least to talk about enjoying, his sexual nature. The reader is free to indulge any fantasy of sexual power, for through sex, one may control others. Ultimately, one may procreate and thus create another; in this, one becomes a prototypical god. Whether or not Panurge in fact marries and gains immortality through physical procreation is extraneous. For the reader, Panurge embodies the feeling of desire for sexual power. Losing the joyous sexual spontaneity he displayed in *Pantagruel,* Panurge becomes an increasingly frightened, inhibited child in *Le Tiers Livre.* Like Adam who covers his body on learning of sin or like the child who learns at a given age that he must not go naked or touch his sexual parts, Panurge sheds his beautiful codpiece and dons brown sack cloth instead. One could interpret this to mean that adult responsibility, traditionally centered around the institution of marriage, is an unnatural state, a learned artifice. This is not to suggest that Panurge resembles Chateaubriand's or Rousseau's "happy savage". Rather, Rabelais calls attention to the fact that the socialization of man is often a painful process running counter to a current deep in human nature. Again, the tension level is maintained in the reader's fantasies; like Panurge he has a will to autonomy even as he seeks to join a group, he too shuns emotional vulnerability at the same time that he makes himself vulnerable.

Finally, Panurge is representative of the spontaneous apprehension of truth, often attributed to children. Because he is unsocialized and unsophisticated, a child often looks beyond or beneath the words and perceives a meaning which reveals the unreality or hypocrisy of a given situation. When one first meets Panurge, he is speaking fourteen languages, many of them gibberish; several interpretations are possible. If Panurge symbolizes a kind of sanity to be found in apparent irrationality, the cryptic languages spoken might point to the fact that language is not the only means by which one communicates and is often an obstacle to conveying meaning.[23] Language is a tool of socialized man.

23. In chapters ix and x of *Gargantua* Rabelais explicitly develops the idea that

J. A. C. Brown cites Freud: "With the acquiring of language cultural indoctrination begins, thought appears."[24] Equally feasible is the idea that Panurge makes his debut by getting the attention of Pantagruel and the reader; he charms, mystifies, confuses, thereby intrigues, and consequently controls. Finally, in a concrete sense, Panurge enters the work as a child seeking the protection of lodging and food. Although he is a man in appearance, he metaphorically communicates his child-like status in the adult world by playing with language, by playing at learning to communicate.

In chapter xxiv of *Pantagruel* Panurge is called upon to give assistance in a matter where discursive reasoning is of no avail. Pantagruel has received from a Parisian lady, whom he had kept as a mistress, a letter addressed: "Au plus aymé des belles, et moins loyal des preux, P.N.T.G.R.L." (*Pantagruel,* 337). Inside there was no writing, only a gold ring, with a flat-cut diamond. Panurge sets about deciphering the hidden meaning in this message. At first, he is sure that some trick will provide the solution; the envelope must contain hidden writing. Fire is created by a combining of nature's elements, thus representing authenticity, naturalness; fittingly, Panurge holds the envelope before a fire to see if some acid had been used that would reveal a message under exposure to fire. Next he tries water, a symbolically purifying natural composite. Having tried a multitude of devices to bring to light hidden writing, but to no avail, he decides that the secret lies in the ring itself. There he finds a message written in Hebrew which means in translation: "Pourquoy me as tu laissé? " (*Pantagruel,* 339). Suddenly Panurge understands: "J'entens le cas. Voyez vous ce dyamant? C'est un dyamant faulx. Telle est doncques l'exposition de ce que veult dire la dame: 'Dy,

language is sometimes an obstacle when one wishes to convey meaning. In these chapters Rabelais reveals language to be an artificial creation which man has used to structure and often control his society. By setting up an apparently logical means for evaluating the symbolic meaning of colors, Rabelais shows that one can reverse traditional meanings which have acquired the status of authority. In the Middle Ages, white symbolized faith (*foye*) and blue stood for steadfastness (*fermeté*). Rabelais proves that white could just as easily symbolize gladness, pleasure, delight (*joye*) and blue could mean heavenly things (*choses celestes*). By illustrating that language has no concrete attachment to things, Rabelais exposes the relativity of traditional ideas. Jean Paris thinks that in chapters ix and x of *Gargantua* Rabelais "voulait néantir le rapport sémantique du signifiant au signifié." Jean Paris, *Hamlet et Panurge* (Paris: Editions du Seuil, 1971), p. 35.

24. J. A. C. Brown, p. 172.

amant faulx, pourquoy me as tu laissé? ' " (*Pantagruel,* 339). This incident in itself is unimportant, just another story where one may laugh at the variety of tricks in Panurge's bag. Yet one might ask, why should Panurge be called upon to explain something to the knowledgeable Pantagruel?

It has been pointed out that Pantagruel is wise in book knowledge, in military procedure and in the ways of social protocol; such wisdom is often gleaned from traditional myths which have acquired the ring of authoritative fact as well as from the discursive process of logical reasoning. Often, refuting traditionally accepted concepts of wisdom, the artist leads his readers into a realm where there is meaning and validity in the truths of feeling and intuition, a realm which may appear irrational and unreal under the scrutiny of civilized logic. Likewise, the child, as pure creature of feeling, may make sense of something which is apparently illogical because of his inability to use discursive logic or to understand the myths of traditional authority. Thus, Panurge teaches Pantagruel when he deciphers the message of the ring as well as when he defeats Thaumaste, revealing that truth may lie beyond the realm of the intellect.

Another example of Panurge's creative trickery triumphing over Pantagruel's logical reasoning is shown in the manner in which the Dipsodes are defeated. In chapter xxvi of *Pantagruel* Panurge advises his friend to cease merry-making and devise a strategy for the impending military bout. Pantagruel comes up with a plan involving two tactics. First, he pretends that in addition to the men with him he has an army at sea that will arrive to assist the following day. Having disclosed this information to the Dipsode prisoner, he also gives him some drugs in the shape of *pastilles* which are to be given to his former compatriots. The prisoner delivers both the message and the *pastilles* to the Dipsodes. Having eaten the *pastilles,* the enemy army is seized by such a powerful, overwhelming thirst that it drinks itself into a state of oblivion. Pantagruel's strategy demands an attack during the night, while the soldiers are too drunk to fight back. Near the enemy camp, Panurge questions Pantagruel's plan: "Seigneur, voulez vous bien faire? Devallez ce vin blanc d'Anjou de la hune et beuvons ici à la bretesque" (*Pantagruel,* 356). When Pantagruel agrees to this momentary diversion, Panurge secretly gives him a drug. As the giant carries out his original plan by first setting the enemy artillery on fire, Panurge's drug begins to act on him; he is seized by such an urge to urinate that he does so, thereby drowning all the men in the enemy camp. What is interesting in this episode is that even though Pantagruel had conceived a seemingly sound plan from a military point of view, Panurge devises a last-minute fool-proof trick, just in case something should go amiss with his friend's strategy. At the death of their soldiers, the three hundred giants decide to counter-attack. Pantagruel is understandably wary, but Panurge assures him that he alone is capable of victory. One suspects, nonetheless, that Panurge is a bit optimistic even for Pantagruel's abilities; fortunately, Loup Garou, captain of the giants, decides to fight Pantagruel alone. The match is still uneven, for Loup Garou has an enchanted club which smashes anything with which it comes into contact. For the first time Pantagruel is insecure and frightened; he prays to God for assistance. At one point when he feels he will lose, he surprises the reader by calling to Panurge for help: "Ha, Panurge, où es tu? " (*Pantagruel,* 363). One might conclude that when Pantagruel is called upon to use intellectual powers such as in the controversy between Baisecul and Humevesne or to display brute force, he is confident and capable. However, when he is up against pretentiousness or trickery (Thaumaste, Loup Garou) or when some mysterious meaning is involved, he looks to Panurge who takes on the proportions of a giant through the indirect means he has devised to compensate for the fact that he is neither an intellectual or physical giant.

Panurge's child-like traits in *Pantagruel* center largely on trickery, natural spontaneity and lack of sexual inhibition. Pantagruel's relationship to him is that of a friend who is enchanted and complimented by being with someone so different from himself. In *Le Tiers Livre* there is a different kind of relationship between these companions – that of wise father and not so wise son. This new relationship is foretold in *Pantagruel.* Alcofrybas steps in to scold Panurge when his fun-making has gone a bit too far. On learning that Panurge has stolen money from the offertory boxes at various cathedrals, Alcofrybas says:

> Voire mais (dis je) vous vous dampnez comme une sarpe et estes larron et sacrilege,– Ouy bien (dist il), comme il vous semble; mais il ne me semble quand à moy: car les pardonnaires me le donnent quand ilz me disent, en presentant les reliques à baiser: "Centuplum accipies". (*Pantagruel,* 308-09)

Finally, exasperated by Panurge's justifications for his behavior, Alcofrybas asks: "Et à quelle fin? dis je. – Mon amy (dist il), tu ne as passe-temps aulcun en ce monde. J'en ay, plus que le Roy, et si vouloys te rais-lier avecques moy, nous ferions diables. – Non, non, (dis je), par sainct Adauras, car tu seras une foys pendu" (*Pantagruel,* 311). In *Le Tiers Livre* Pantagruel is explicit about his disapproval of Panurge's irresponsibility.

Having conquered Dipsodia, Pantagruel assigns various sectors for wardenship. To Panurge he gives Salmagundia:

> Et se gouverna si bien et prudentement Monsieur le nouveau chastellain qu'en moins de quartorze jours il dilapida le revenu certain et incertain de sa chastellenie pour troys ans. Non proprement dilapida, comme vous pourriez dire en fondations de monasteres, erections de temples, bastimens de collieges et hospitaulx, ou jectant son lard aux chiens, mais despendit en mille petitz bancquetz et festins joyeulx ouvers à tous venens, mesmement tous bons compaignons, jeunes fillettes et mignonnes gualoises, abastant boys, bruslant les grosses souches pour la vente des cendres, prenent argent d'avance, achaptant cher, vendent à bon marché, et mangeant son bled en herbe. (*Le Tiers Livre*, 410)

Motivated by concern for his spendthrift friend's future, Pantagruel points out that if he does not learn to be less generous, he will never be rich. The desire to be rich in this world is not his goal, Panurge says, for he prefers to live for the pleasure of the moment. This sort of inability to conceive of, much less plan for, the future is characteristic of a child. Yet Panurge is only an emotional child, for his rationalizations belong to the province of adult reasoning. His behavior can be explained, he says, by the four cardinal virtues; although his arguments reverse civilized economic theory, they are logically sound explanations of his philosophy. First, one must always take money in advance if he wishes to be prudent, for one may die tomorrow. In other words, he does not save, nor does he give credit to anyone. Secondly, he himself must buy expensive things on credit and sell them cheap so that he may have ready cash. And this cash must be used to provide feasts for good friends and pretty young girls. The last two principles are extensions of the Robin Hood image that Panurge often projects when questioned about the unorthodoxy of his life style. Thirdly, he must get rid of wild animals, thieves and murderers. In other words, his own dishonesty is actually a good thing, for the money he takes from others enables him to rid the world of truly dangerous and truly dishonest people. Finally, by being temperate himself, he may save a little with which to help those who are sick or distressed. Pantagruel replies that he understands the attitude which proclaims that only joyous, free-spirited persons may spend so much in so little time; nonetheless, he would prefer that Panurge forego his rationalizations and try to live in a more socialized manner (*Le Tiers Livre*, 410-14). In the next chapter, Pantagruel somewhat out of patience, demands to know when his friend will be out of debt. It is the father insisting that his son not always remain in a state of dependence, that he become a responsible adult. "Jamais" is Panurge's answer: "Es calendes grecques, respondit Panurge, ors que tout le monde sera content, et que serez heritier de vous mesmes. Dieu me guarde d'en estre hors" (*Le Tiers Livre*, 415). Panurge's explanation, in praise of debtors, is a lyric poem which glorifies the state of childhood, the state without responsibilities or problems.

Before considering the implications of this lengthy speech which covers chapters iii, iv and v, one should examine some critical opinions of the form. Various genres in popular usage in the sixteenth century are offered in explanation. Some critics call it paradox, others panegyric, others satiric eulogy and others say pure lyricism. According to a dictionary definition, paradox means: "A statement seemingly absurd or contradictory, yet in fact true; A statement essentially self-contradictory, false, or absurd."[25] More specifically, a paradox was a literary genre, so popular in the Renaissance period that it rivaled the epigram and the sonnet.[26] One might consider Panurge's *éloge* of debtors and borrowers a paradox inasmuch as the debtor's superiority is a ridiculous idea; but, Panurge pleads so well, in a rhetoric so noble and eloquent that one is almost convinced that he is speaking truth, even though the premise seems false:

> Representez vous un monde autre, on quel un chascun preste, un chascun doibve, tous soient debteurs, tous soient presteurs. O quelle harmonie sera parmy les réguliers mouvemens des cieulz .... Entre les humains, paix, amour, dilection, fidelité, repous, banquetz, festins, joye, liesse, or, argent, menue monnoie, chaisnes, bagues, marchandises troteront de main en main. Nul procès, nulle guerre, nul debat; nul n'y sera usurier, nul leschart, nul chichart, nul refusant. Vray Dieu, ne sera ce l'aage d'or, le regne de Saturne? (*Le Tiers Livre*, 420-21)

Paradox functions much like satire, for in it the author may hide some message ("truth") about his view of man and life under the guise of playing with words. It is thus appropriate that Panurge express the paradoxical idea, for he is a character both enigmatic and paradoxical. As a misfit, as a kind of child, he can simultaneously oppose and expose the fallacies in traditional concepts.

In another feasible interpretation of the *éloge*, Panurge is Rabelais's alter-ego; Rabelais, growing old, was perhaps weary of pandering to the nobility to try to win protection and approval. Possibly, the fantasy of

---

25. *Funk & Wagnalls Standard College Dictionary*, eds., Shelia C. Brantley, Olga Coren, Samuel Davis (Chicago: Harcourt, Brace & World, Inc., 1968), p. 977.

26. A. E. Malloch, "The Techniques and Function of the Renaissance Paradox," pp. 191-203 in *Studies in Philology*, LIII (Chapel Hill: The University of North Carolina Press, 1956), p. 191.

a secure world where he could relax and freely depend on others was attractive to him. From another point of view, Leo Spitzer sees the *éloge* as an example of lyric poetry, and added proof that Rabelais's art is based on a kind of lyric fantasy.[27] Alfred Glauser agrees with Spitzer's view, calling the *éloge* an example of "art pur".[28] Panurge in *Le Tiers Livre* is still in control of himself and his environment, although he has begun to become insecure as revealed by his constant questioning and doubting. In defending himself against his growing insecurity, perhaps he creates the *éloge,* a delicate, radiant poem proposing a universal theory of happiness, in order to rationalize his desire for an evaporating personal utopia.

By placing the *éloge* at the beginning of *Le Tiers Livre*, Rabelais establishes a different character "set" for Panurge. First, one sees that Panurge will try to control his world by different methods from those used in *Pantagruel.* Persuasion and verbal eloquence replace tricks and spontaneous joy. Glauser says that Rabelais is more sure of his artistic ability to use language convincingly in *Le Tiers Livre* and thus places the *éloge* at the beginning to indicate that "la négation de la vie et la prédominance de la parole" will subsequently be the essence of Panurge.[29] Secondly, a different relationship is established between Panurge and Pantagruel. No longer so easily charmed, Pantagruel rejects his friend's eloquent plea and chastises him in the manner of an irate parent:

J'entends (respondit Pantagruel) et me semblez bon topicqueur et affecté à vostre cause. Mais prechez et patrocinez d'icy à la Pentecoste, en fin vous serez esbahy comment rien ne me aurez persuadé, et par vostre beau parler, je ne me ferez entrer en debtes. Rien (dict le sainct Envoyé) à personne de doibvez, fors amours et dilection mutuelle. Vous me usez icy de belles graphides et diatyposes, et me plaisent très bien: mais je vous diz que, si figurez un affronteur efronté et importun emprunteur entrant de nouveau en une ville ja advertie de ses meurs, vous trouverez que à son entrée plus seront les citoyens en effroy et trepidation, que si la Peste y entroit en habillement tel que la trouva le philosophe Tyanien dedans Ephese. Et suys d'opinion que ne erroient les Perses, estimans le second vice estre mentir: le premier estre debvoir. Car debtes et mensonges sont ordinairement ensemble ralliez.(*Le Tiers Livre*, 424-25)

27. Leo Spitzer, "Le Prétendu Réalisme de Rabelais," pp. 139-50 in *Modern Philology*, IIIVII (Chicago: The University of Chicago Press, 1940), p. 148.

28. Alfred Glauser, *Rabelais créateur* (Paris: Editions A.-G. Nizet, 1966), p. 158.

29. Glauser, p. 131.

His final admonishment is that it is a disgrace to owe to someone who has worked for his money and that Panurge must never again acquire debts. To insure a new start, Pantagruel absolves him from his present debts.

From the moment Panurge loses the security of childhood dependence, he seems to become an actor. Glauser emphasizes that Panurge is always an actor: "Le monde pour Panurge est un théâtre; sa morale aussi est celle d'un comédien. Ses actions ne sont justifiées que si elles sont vues; il luy faut, comme à Rabelais, un public."[30] Panurge is perpetually an actor insofar as he assumes the role of comedian. However, the Panurge who amuses the public is playing a role which is natural to a child, that of attention getting; in this context he is not acting. From the beginning of *Le Tiers Livre* he makes an effort to play an unnatural role, that of adult. When actors assume identities other than their own, they don the appropriate clothing. Panurge, to accustom himself to his new role, symbolically changes his manner of dress. Children have always "dressed up" to imitate the adult they have not yet become, to play at being grown up. Huizinga says:

> The "differentness" and secrecy of play are most vividly expressed in "dressing up". Here the "extraordinary" nature of play reaches perfection. The disguised or masked individual "plays" another part, another being. He *is* another being. The terrors of childhood, openhearted gaiety, mystic fantasy and sacred awe are all inextricably entangled in this strange business of masks and disguises.[31]

As an emotional child, Panurge wears no mask, yet paradoxically he functions as a mask which the reader may put on in order subjectively to act out his own fantasies. The reader can more easily identify with Panurge's "make-believe" than with that of a real child precisely because Panurge is disguised as an adult. Reader and character, thus, enter a subjective pact made possible and thereby objectified by the work.

In the beginning of *Le Tiers Livre* Panurge exchanges his magnificent, fashionable clothes for plain, simple garb:

> Au lendemain Panurge se feit perser l'aureille dextre à la judaique, et y atacha un petit anneau d'or à ouvraige de tauchie, on caston duquel estoit une pusse enchassée . . . . Print quatre aulnes de bureau: s'en acoustra comme d'une robbe longue à simple cousture; desista porter le hault de ses chausses, et attacha des lunettes à

30. Glauser, p. 131.

31. Johan Huizinga, *Homo Ludens: A Study of the Play-Element in Culture* (Boston: The Beacon Press, 1950), p. 13.

son bonnet. En tel estat se praesenta davant Pantagruel, lequel trouva le desguise-
ment estrange, mesmemént ne voyant plus sa belle et magnifique braguette, en
laquelle il souloit comme en l'ancre sacré constituer son dernier refuge contre
tous naufraiges d'adversité. (*Le Tiers Livre,* 430)

Pantagruel, mystified, asks how Panurge hopes to attract a suitable wife
dressed so strangely:

Mais ce n'est la guise des amoureux, ainsi avoir bragues avalades, et laisser pendre
sa chemise sur les genoilx sans hault de chausses, avecques robbe longue de
bureau, qui est couleur inusitée en robbes talares entre gens de bien et de vertus.
(*Le Tiers Livre,* 431)

Panurge explains:

La couleur, respondit Panurge, est aspre aux potz, à propos, c'est mon bureau, je
le veulx dorenavant tenir et de près reguarder à mes affaires. Puys qu'une fois je
suis quitte [i.e., out of debt], vous ne veistes oncques homme plus mal plaisant
que je seray, si Dieu ne me ayde. (*Le Tiers Livre,* 431)

Panurge's verbal protest (*l'éloge*) against accepting adult responsibility
has been to no avail. Rather than risk rejection by Pantagruel, the
symbolic father, Panurge capitulates saying he will do what his friend
wishes and will even go so far as to marry. Yet he must emphasize his
unwillingness to adopt this role; thus, he dons a dull, ugly costume, his
image of the role he is about to assume. One could compare this change
of clothes to an initiation ceremony where a young boy admits publicly
that he is now a man; he must play a role before the public in spite of
the fact that true maturity has nothing to do with such a formality.
Still, the new costume is not a suitable admission of manhood. Pantagruel protests, not only because the outfit is unbecoming, but also
because it is not a socially acceptable manner of dress. It is the traditional father disapproving of his son's symbolic rebellion. And Panurge's decision to marry is as much a pretense to adulthood as is his
inappropriate costume. If Panurge were emotionally prepared to lose
the uniqueness of being a child, he would find a wife and Rabelais
would terminate his work or develop it in another direction. Inasmuch
as Panurge is neither ready nor capable of acting on the new role to
which he pays lip service, he continues to leave the responsibility for
controlling his life to others. In *Pantagruel* the responsibility delegated
to others was that of physical protection (food, shelter, clothing). In *Le
Tiers Livre* he places on others a much more complex burden, that of
making for him decisions he cannot make. Everything, in *Le Tiers
Livre,* is carried out under the pretext that Panurge has truly changed;
he is no longer the childish trickster of the *Pantagruel,* but a man

tormented by doubt. Nonetheless, he is essentially the same character. Pantagruel continues to protect him, acting now as emotional guide and counselor. In the role of patient father, Pantagruel gives his own answers to the questions posed by his unsure friend, but insists at the same time that Panurge find the answers that are suitable to him:

> Vostre conseil (dist Panurge) soubs correction, semble à la chanson de Ricochet. Ce ne sont que sarcasmes, mocqueries, es redictes contradictoires. Les unes destruisent les aultres. Je ne sçay es quelles me tenir. — Aussi (respondit Pantagruel) en vos propositions tant y a de si et de mais, que je n'y sçaurois rien fonder ne rien resouldre. N'estez vous asceuré de vostre vouloir? Le poinct principal y gist: tout le reste est fortuit, et dependent des fatales dispositions du ciel . . . . Il se y convient mettre à l'adventure, les oeilz bandez, baissant la teste, baisant la terre et se recommandant à Dieu au demourant, puys qu'une foys l'on se y veult mettre. Aultre asceurance ne vous en sçauroys je donner. (*Le Tiers Livre*, 440-41)

A philosophical lesson to be learned from *Le Tiers Livre* is that absolute truth does not exist. One must learn to find his own concept of truth by questioning and doubting. Emotionally, one grows more mature by coming to understand his own needs and wants and by adjusting these to the society he lives in as best he can. One may say, then, that Panurge's quest for a suitable wife is a stylistic pretext to intellectual and emotional truths which Rabelais wishes to convey. He is chosen because he is the least socialized, the least traditional, thus the least marriageable character in the work. This gives Rabelais free rein to develop his work in any direction his own ever-changing thoughts and needs may dictate.

Panurge has no woman in mind in spite of his incessant talk about sexual conquests. When sexually rebuffed by the only woman he ever mentions in terms of love, he flees for fear of a beating (*Pantagruel*, 331). If one poses an ideal of marriage as a relationship in which two individuals are united on several levels, then, Panurge as a symbolized incarnation of egotism would not have the least idea of how one harmonizes with another person. Then, his hesitation and his fears of marriage reflect his own incapacity rather than his inability to find a virtuous woman. One can even suggest that *Le Tiers Livre* offers a lesson in common sense: one must have some knowledge of oneself as an emotional being before one is able to participate in adult society. Panurge as a mature adult would have been able to make a decision, be it positive or negative; on the contrary, he remains in the limbo of indecision. In some ways his dilemma is worse that that of an actual child who is somewhat bound to the decisions made for him by others. Physically and mentally Panurge functions as an adult and can consequently question all the decisions which he urges others to make for him. This is the plight of the emotionally immature adult, unfree to the degree that he is not psychologically independent. Panurge, in *Le Tiers Livre,* finding no answer among the specialists of his own country, must make a choice to abandon his quest or continue it elsewhere.

Le Tiers Livre seems to be structurally divided into two parts by chapter ix which serves as the conclusion of the statement of the problem and the introduction to its resolution. Stylistically, chapter ix is pivotal: Panurge poses the problem question: "Should I marry? " and Pantagruel provides the solution, "No, you should not or Yes, you should". Chapter x begins the search for a wife for Panurge; the pretense of a solution lies in the concrete fact of the quest. Ultimately, however, *Le Tiers Livre* is not truly divided, for the whole book becomes a paradox in which there is problem and solution and at the same time no problem and no solution, with the ninth chapter as a microcosm of this rhythm. Again, the conflict/resolution pattern is maintained in form as well as through character. In keeping with the idea that the *éloge* of chapters iii through v belongs to the then popular genre of paradox, chapter ix and finally the whole book become an extended use of that genre. One might better understand the development of the paradox through antithetical linguistic structure by comparing chapter ix to a musical composition.

The composition is formed by verse and refrain. The principal melody of the verse is alternately executed in major and minor key. The refrain is counterpoint to the main melody. The words which accompany the melody are the theme of *Le Tiers Livre,* the "Should I marry" expressed by Panurge. When Panurge declares his desire to marry, the tune is in a major key and his protestations against marriage denote the minor key. When Panurge asks for advice on his decision to marry, Pantagruel replies that since he has already decided, all that remains is to do it, but Panurge insists on his friend's opinion anyway. What follows is a series of antithetical repetitions with Pantagruel's interjections fixing the refrain:

— Voyre mais (dist Panurge) je ne la vouldrois exécuter sans vostre conseil et bon advis.
— J'en suis (respondit Pantagruel) d'advis, et vous le conseille.
— Mais (dist Panurge) si vous congnoissiez, que mon meilleur feust tel que je suys demeurer, sans entreprendre cas de nouvelleté, j'aymerois mieulx ne me marier poinct.

— Poinct doncques ne vous mariez, respondit Pantagruel.

— Voire mais (dist Panurge) vouldriez vous qu'ainsi seulet je demeurasse toute ma vie sans compaignie conjugale? Vous sçavez qu'il est escript: *veh soli*. L'homme seul n'a jamais tel soulas qu'on veoyd entre gens mariez.

— Mariez-vous doncq, de par Dieu, respondit Pantagruel.

— Mais si (dist Panurge) ma femme me faisoit coqu, comme vous sçavez qu'il en est grande année, ce seroit assez pour me faire trespasser hors les gonds de patience. (*Le Tiers Livre*, 437-38)

The echo technique of this composition fixes the tone for the repetitious, paradoxical, circular structure of *Le Tiers Livre*; and the form parallels the paradoxical message that in life there is only quest with no absolute resolution.

The quest wends its way through various potential resolutions: there are answers sought randomly in Virgil, a series of visits to both traditional and unconventional authorities of the day and finally a voyage so strange that Panurge's plight becomes secondary. Seeking a definite answer which is never provided creates tension, a sense of frustration and futility. Lest the reader become bored with the tedium of this repetitively exaggerated lesson in metaphysics, Rabelais continues all the while to entertain, engaging one's wits through his use of polemic, startling one's imagination in his portrayal of fantastic, bizarre humans and finally sustaining one's laughter by means of his comic creation, Panurge. The last forty-three chapters of *Le Tiers Livre* describe Panurge's quest. The various signs given in answer to Panurge's question are interpreted negatively by Pantagruel and positively by Panurge. For example, Pantagruel advises Panurge to seek an answer by throwing dice to find a line number on a page of Virgil that has been selected at random. The line reads: "Nec Deus hunc mensa, Dea nec dignata cubili est. Digne ne feut d'estre en table du dieu, Et n'eut on lict de la déesse lieu" (*Le Tiers Livre*, 447). The meaning construed by Pantagruel is that Panurge's wife will cuckold him and will be a whore as well, whereas Panurge's understanding of the message is that his wife will be beautiful like the goddess Venus, but not a whore, and that he himself is unlike the poor man who got himself cuckolded. The line reversed indicates that his wife will be chaste, modest, faithful and not rebellious. In chapter xiv Panurge and Pantagruel repeat the pattern of the interchange just described. In a dream Panurge sees his pretty, young wife make two horns to go above his forehead and then she turns into an owl and he a drum. According to Pantagruel, the horns mean that his friend will be cuckolded, the drum means that she will beat her husband and the owl represents one who is by nature a thief. Stubbornly affirming his illusion of having an impenetrable ego, Panurge reads the horns as symbolic of the horn of abundance or the horns of satyrs, men so sexually potent that they would never be cuckolded. The drum signifies that he is jolly and the owl that she is neat and dainty. This same pattern of interaction between the odd couple is repeated in multiple variations, like variations on a musical theme: a fortune teller, a deaf mute, a poet, an astrologer, a theologian, a physician, a philosopher, a fool and a lawyer give paradoxical answers which must consequently be deciphered.

It seems that Panurge and Pantagruel are caught in a situation of playing devil's advocate to each other. Although Pantagruel has succinctly stated that Panurge must make his own decision, he nonetheless makes every effort to influence these decisions by stating his own views. While Panurge does not accept the authority of his companion's opinions, he still remains indecisive by staying optimistic enough to retain the possibility of choice. From one perspective, Pantagruel is further reduced to the human level in this interaction. In *Pantagruel* he was unerring in providing his friend with a sense of security; in *Le Tiers Livre* his powers are not strong enough to calm Panurge's fears or to answer his questions. Plattard explains this change of character by saying that Rabelais was tired of describing giants:

> Pantagruel, à vrai dire, laissait la première place à Panurge. Le conteur était las, probablement, de revenir sur la description de la stature, de la force et de l'appétit du géant. Déjà dans le *Gargantua*, le thème "gigantal" était fréquemment négligé. Dans le *Tiers Livre*, il n'est plus du tout question d' "horribles et épouvantables prouesses". Le titre annonce plus modestement des "faits et dicts héroïques de Pantagruel". Encore y chercherait-on vainement des exploits de héros. Le géant n'est engagé dans aucune guerre. Sa force prodigieuse, inutile est passée sous silence. Le conteur omet d'attirer notre attention sur l'énormité de ses géants . . . L'interêt du récit est ailleurs: il est concentré sur Panurge.[32]

One might further elucidate the scholarly problem of Pantagruel's character change by suggesting that while Pantagruel is superhuman, a giant in terms of physical strength and in intellectual knowledge, in the realm of emotional knowledge he is but a man, seeking to help a friend, although not certain just what to say or do. A stylistic explanation sheds further light on the change. In *Le Tiers Livre* Pantagruel is used as a buffer to Panurge's questions and thus as a catalyst to Rabelais's philosophical meanderings. Finally, in light of the view of Panurge as an

32. Jean Plattard. *François Rabelais* (Paris: Boivin & Cie, 1932), p. 242.

emotional child, Pantagruel is the father figure who tries to give wise answers while letting his child learn from experience, yet he is often unable to resist proffering dogmatic opinions. In this role, Pantagruel reads the advice given by the poet, Raminagrobis, which says in essence that in matters of marriage each man must be his own judge; he then reprimands Panurge: "Telle a tousjours esté mon opinion, et autant vous en diz la premiere foys que m'en parlastez; mais vous en mocquiez tacitement, il m'en soubvient, et coignois que philautie et amour de soy vous deçoit. Faisons aultrement" (*Le Tiers Livre*, 526). It sounds as if Pantagruel is angry with himself for giving Panurge the interpretations which are so constantly rejected.

Stylistically, Panurge refuses to accept the negative views of his possible marriage, in order that the philosophical quest remain open. As child-like character, he refuses because he is not emotionally ready to submit to traditional answers. In *Le Tiers Livre* Panurge is paradoxically more adult and more child than in the *Pantagruel*; the step toward growth brought about by doubt and insecurity contradictorily makes him act like a dependent child who has lost the ability to act. On the one hand, he is confused by the difficulty of paradoxical answers given him, such as Raminagrobis's poem:

> Prenez la, ne la prenez pas
> Si vous la prenez, c'est bien faict.
> Si ne la prenez en effect,
> ᑎe sera oeuvré par compas.
> ᑕualoppez, mais allez le pas.
> Recullez, entrez y de faict.
>   Prenez-la, ne.
> Jeusnez, prenez double repas.
> Defaictez ce qu'estoit refaict.
> Refaictez ce qu'estoit defaict.
> Soubhaytez luy vie et trespas.
>   Prenez la, ne. (*Le Tiers Livre*, 490-91)

Panurge responds in frustration: "Par la response qu'il nous donne, je suys aussi saige que oncques puis ne fourneasmes nous" (*Le Tiers Livre*, 493). On the other hand, at the same time that Panurge seems too bewildered to grasp what is happening to him, he perceives with the intuitive honesty of a child that much of intellectual double-talk is removed from real life: to understand something intellectually is not to resolve it for there still remain the feelings about it to be dealt with. At the end of chapter xxxv Pantagruel speaks for a rational view:

— Je interprete (dist Pantagruel) avoir et n'avoir femme en ceste façon: que femme avoir est l'avoir à usaige tel que Nature la créa, qui est pour l'ayde, esbatement et societé de l'homme; n'avoir femme est ne soy apoiltronner autour d'elle, pour elle ne contaminer celle unicque et supreme affection que doibt l'homme à Dieu; ne laisser les offices qu'il doibt naturellement à sa patrie, à la Republique, à ses amys; ne mettre en non chaloir ses estudes et negoces, pour continuellement à sa femme complaire. Prenant en ceste maniere avoir et n'avoir femme, je ne voids repugnance ne contradiction es termes. (*Le Tiers Livre,* 551-52)

Panurge's response is a plea for recognition of the irrational, asocial, feeling side of man:

Vous dictez d'orgues (respondit Panurge) mais je croy que je suis descendu on puiz tenebreux, onquel disoit Heraclytus estre Verité cachée. Je ne voy goutte, je n'entends rien, je sens mes sens tous hebetez, et doubte grandement que je soye charmé. (*Le Tiers Livre,* 552)

Since Panurge has found no resolution for his problem among the specialists of his own country, he must abandon the quest or continue it elsewhere. Since he can neither return to the carefree childhood world portrayed in *Pantagruel,* nor decide to attach himself to the adult world through the symbol of marriage, he chooses to continue his search on foreign terrain. Panurge in *Le Quart Livre* is both the aggressive, sadistic character of *Pantagruel* and the insecure, uncontrolled character of *Le Tiers Livre.* The extreme lack of control which Panurge manifests in *Le Quart Livre* seems to occur when he loses Pantagruel's support. In this book Pantagruel cannot be supportive of his friend's physical needs, as in *Pantagruel,* nor of his emotional needs, as in *Le Tiers Livre,* because of the existence of natural phenomena which he himself cannot control (storms, a whale). In addition, they are traveling among islands inhabited by strange creatures with whom they have no idea of how to interact or of what to expect. Still in France, questioning familiar types of people, Pantagruel could act as a wise father and concerned friend. Having left the security of familiarity, Pantagruel must find his own ways to face the unknown and thus can do nothing for Panurge.

Panurge seems to become a caricature even of himself, all his traits exaggerated to an extreme. Sadistic fun-making becomes total cruelty when he causes the death of Dindenault. This particular act of barbarity is directly associated with his fear of sexual inadequacy. The quarrel with Dindenault begins with a comment that Panurge's costume is strange and that he looks like a fine figure of a cuckold. In keeping with his inability to engage in physical action shown in *Le Tiers Livre,* Panurge reacts with a verbal assault, telling the sheep merchant to be careful lest he cuckold him. Angered, the merchant takes a sword to Panurge

whose bravado turns into the cowardly fear of a child who has·taunted
a comrade, but runs to his mother when self defense becomes necessar-
y; Panurge runs to Pantagruel for protection, while Frère Jan is ready to
do battle with Dindenault. In chapter vi Panurge becomes once again
bold and approaches the sheep dealer on the pretext of making a friend-
ly business offer; he asks to buy a sheep. Still treating Panurge like a
fool, Dindenault says he is funny looking and laughingly calls him
"Robin mouton". Becoming increasingly abusive, Dindenault tells Panurge that he is unworthy to buy so fine a sheep and he ends with the
final taunt that Panurge is a cuckold. As if this sadistic teasing were his
price for striking a bargain, the merchant then sells Panurge a sheep
which Panurge throws into the sea, knowing the flock will follow and
Dindenault as well. And thus Panurge vents the pent up anger of a
person who feels helpless, ineffectual and impotent and can only make
his frustration felt by some extreme act of destruction.

Glauser finds two possibilities for Rabelais's having chosen to include this episode in his work. From a stylistic point of view: "Panurge
est actif dans cet épisode avant d'être passif dans celui de la tempê-
te."[33] Secondly, Panurge functions in the work as a pretense for comedy; the Dindenault incident could be found extremely funny:

> C'est le comique essentiel de Panurge: une cause futile des résultats immenses.
> Dans une société qui nierait les droits du comique, Panurge serait arrêté. Il y a
> dans l'histoire de sa vie de quoi être emprisonné à vie. Mais, dans l'oeuvre tout est
> permis.[34]

And if one views Panurge as emotional child, one could say that this
episode represents his final attempt to gain control of his surroundings
and of himself. He explains his action, thus:

> Jamais homme ne me feist plaisir sans recompense, ou recongnoissance pour le
> moins. Je ne suys point ingrat et ne le feuz, ne seray. Jamais homme ne me feist
> desplaisir sans repentence, ou en ce monde, ou en l'autre. Je ne suys poinct fat
> jusques là.[35]

From this time, Panurge makes no further pretense of being adult or of
wanting to be accepted in the adult world.

In chapter xviii Panurge loses complete control of himself for the
first time when he realizes that he may perish in the storm at sea and

33. Glauser, p. 144.
34. Glauser, p. 144.
35. Rabelais, *Le Quart Livre, Oeuvres complètes*, vol. II, ed., Pierre Jourda
(Paris: Editions Garnier Frères, 1962), p. 58.

that no one can help him. His reaction is that of a hysterical child who has not yet learned that life's misfortunes demand a kind of stoic calm in order that chaos not prevail:

> Panurge, ayant du contenu en son estomach bien repeu les poissons scatophages, restoit acropy sus le tillac, tout affligé, tout meshaigné, et à demy mort; invocqua tous les benoistz saincts et sainctes à son ayde, protesta de soy confesser en temps et lieu. (*Le Quart Livre*, 94)

He resembles a little boy who believes that if he says he is sorry for his misdeeds, he will be saved by God or by his parents from impending disaster, but when this does not work, he regresses to an infantile state:

> Bebebe bous, bous, bous! Voyez à la calamite de vostre boussole, de grace, maistre Astrophile, dont nous vient ce fortunal. Par ma foy, j'ai belle paour. Bou, bou, bou, bous, bous. C'est faict de moy. Je me conchie de male raige de paour. Bou, bou, bou, bou! Otto to to to to ti! Otto, to to to to ti! Bou bou bou, ou ou ou bou bou bous bous! Je naye, je naye, je meurs. Bonnes gens, je naye. (*Le Quart Livre*, 96)

In the following chapter the crew members do what they can to keep their ship from sinking. Meanwhile, Panurge squats in a corner weeping and moaning. Falling back on the devious trickery practiced in *Pantagruel,* he tries to bargain, saying he will give a lot of money to anyone who will put him ashore. When Frère Jan swears at his blubbering companion, berating him for his cowardice, Panurge pleads with him not to offend God. Not being able to depend on his symbolic father, Pantagruel, for physical protection, he turns instead to God's representative, a spiritual father, begging Frère Jan to pray for him and even trying to bribe him with promises of building him a chapel if he will but help. In chapter xx Panurge decides that he must make a will. Epistemon gently rebukes him and adds that if he drowns, so will his projected document:

> — Quelque bonne vague, respondit Panurge, le jectera à bourt comme feist Ulyxes; et quelque fille de Roy, allant à l'esbat sur le serain, le rencontrera, puis le fera tres bien executer, et près le rivaige me fera eriger quelque magnificque cenotaphe, comme feist Dido à son mary Sychée. (*Le Quart Livre*, 103)

The reader might simply accept Panurge's hysterical reaction of fear as something that could happen to anyone. But, it is difficult to identify with the blatant egotism of this last remark. Only a child, or a neurotic, unconscious yet of the feelings and rights of others, could be so totally self-concerned. Nonetheless, the reader will probably recognize, consciously or not, the immediate human impulse to save oneself at all cost.

After the storm has passed, Panurge regains his gay manner and even has the audacity to scold the others for not having worked hard enough during the storm. When they touch land, he is the first one off the boat. Safety assured, Panurge can explain: "De paour, je n'en ay poinct, quant est de moy: je m'appelle Guillaume sans paour. De couraige, tant et plus. Je ne entends couraige de brebis: je diz couraige de loup, asceurance de meurtrier. Et ne crains rien, que les dangiers" (*Le Quart Livre*, 111). In other words, Panurge fears nothing as long as he is in control of the situation. For example, he is not much frightened by the monsters on the islands, for they are not hostile and if necessary, his friends can protect him on land.[36]

Pantagruel returns to his role of comforter and protector in chapter xxiii. Having sighted a whale, the crew prepares to do battle. Panurge's reaction is predictably fright and cowardice, and he moans:

Nous sommes tous perduz. O que pour l'occire praesentement feust icy quelque vaillant Perseus!
— Persé jus par moy sera, respondit Pantagruel. N'ayez paour.
— Vertus Dieu, dist Panurge, faictes que soyons hors les causes de paour. Quand voulez vous que j'aye paour, sinon quand le dangier est evident? (*Le Quart Livre*, 138)

As good as his word, Pantagruel slays the whale. One could view this incident as a parallel to the good parent's coming to a child, frightened in the night by some dream, to reassure him that his monsters are not real and thus cannot hurt him.

Through the rest of *Le Quart Livre* Panurge behaves like a terrified child to the point that he bears no resemblance to the character who helped Pantagruel fight armies in *Pantagruel.* In face of impending battle, in chapter xxxvii Panurge tries to avoid fighting by offering first to run an errand and then to pray while the others defeat the enemy. And, in chapter lv he lapses into a hysterical tirade when the crew comes upon the unexplainable phenomenon of the frozen words. Later, as

---

36. Modern psychology gives explanations for characteristic behavior of a child who feels deserted by a parent or an authority figure. According to Freud: "A child in its greed for love does not enjoy having to share the affection of its parents with its brothers and sisters; and it notices that the whole of their affection is lavished upon it once more whenever it arouses their anxiety by falling ill. It has now discovered a means of enticing out its parents' love . . . . Illnesses of this kind are the result of intention. They are as a rule levelled at a particular person." Sigmund Freud, *Dora: An Analysis of a Case of Hysteria* (New York: Collier Books, 1966), p. 61.

they approach the island of thieves, Panurge is even more out of control than previously. He is sure they are all going to be killed and eaten. His fear in this instance is particularly interesting, for in *Pantagruel* he was proud of being a thief and in *Le Tiers Livre* he glorifies those who take from others in the *éloge paradoxal.* Possibly his insecurity is now so great that he is threatened by any resemblance to himself which might diminish his uniqueness in the group. Panurge slinks off into the store room when his friends laugh at his fears. In a spirit of fun-making the crew fires a gun salute to the island. Startled by the noise, Panurge:

> comme un boucq estourdy, sort de la soutte en chemise, ayant seulement un demy bas de chausses en jambe, sa barbe toute mouschetée de miettes de pain, tenent en main un grand chat soubelin, attaché à l'aultre demy bas be ses chausses. Et remuant les babines comme un cinge qui cherche poulz en teste, tremblant et clacquetant des dens, se tira vers frere Jan, lequel estoit assis sus le porte-haubant de tribort, et devotement le pria avoir de luy compassion, et le tenir en saulveguarde de son bragmart; affermant et jurant, par sa part de Papimanie, qu'il avoit à heure praesente veu tous les diables deschainez. (*Le Quart Livre,* 244)

Looking and acting like a madman, Panurge loses control of his body as well as of his emotions:

> Frere Jan à l'approcher sentoit je ne sçay quel odeur aultre que de la pouldre à canon. Dont il tira Panurge en place, et apperceut que sa chemise estoit toute foyreuse et embrenée de frays. La vertus retentrice du nerf qui restrainct le muscle nommé sphincter (c'est le trou du cul) estoit dissolue par la vehemence de paour qu'il avoit eu en ses phantasticques visions. (*Le Quart Livre,* 245)

The happy, dynamic Panurge of *Pantagruel* has evolved from a state of untiring activity and unbounded gaiety to a condition of total immobility and fear. Alan Watts expressses the opinion that: "The total restraint of movement is the equivalent of total doubt, of refusal to trust one's senses or feelings."[37] The unrealistically confident child of *Pantagruel* has progressed to realistic doubt in *Le Tiers Livre*: from there he may become either an adult capable of coping with fears and unpleasant realities or he may remain an unrealistic child as does Panurge. Unfortunately, now aware of frightening forces in his world, but unable to cope with them, Panurge regresses to total doubt in a kind of catatonic negation of the self.

When Frère Jan sees Panurge's plight, he calls Pantagruel to observe

---

37. Alan Watts, *The Book: On the Taboo Against Knowing Who You Are* (New York: Pantheon Books, 1966), pp. 37-38.

their friend, covered with excrement and clutching a cat which has scratched him to shreds. Pantagruel has no sympathy: "Allez, dist Pantagruel, allez, de par Dieu, vous estuver, vous nettoyer, vous asceurer, prendre chemise blanche, et vous revister" (*Le Quart Livre,* 248). At this scolding, Panurge bounces back to his former, gay self thus maintaining the conflict/resolution rhythm:

> Dictez vous, respondit Panurge, que j'ay paour? Pas maille. Je suys, par la vertus Dieu, plus couraigeux que si j'eusse autant de mousches avallé qu'il en est mis en paste dedans Paris, depuys la feste S. Jan jusques à la Toussains. Ha, ha, ha! Houay! Que diable est cecy? Appelez vous cecy foyre, bren, crottes, merde, fiant, dejection, matiere fecale, excrement, repaire, laisse, esmeut, fumée, estron, scybale ou spyrathe? C'est, croy je, sapphran d'Hibernie. Ho, ho, hie! C'est sapphran d'Hibernie! Sela! Beuvons. (*Le Quart Livre,* 248)

This reply is an affirmation of the goodness of asocial, natural man. Offensive waste matter is transformed into the dearest of spices. The final word of the last book which critics are certain Rabelais wrote is "Beuvons". It is appropriate that comic, ridiculous Panurge repeat Rabelais's message to all life's woes, which says in essence that one must look to his natural, sensual self; one must laugh and "drink up."

Having looked at Panurge's child-like characteristics in *Pantagruel, Le Tiers Livre* and *Le Quart Livre,* one can make some suppositions as to why Rabelais would have created such a character. One might say that Pantagruel cast in the role of father is representative of Rabelais, raising the legitimate son he never had. The giants, Gargantua and Pantagruel, could never have been Rabelais's sons even though he directs them from infancy to maturity, for they belong to his intellectual side. In the case of Gargantua, Rabelais places himself against scholastic education; through Pantagruel he indicates that he is in favor of the humanist education of the Renaissance. In this sense, one can say that Gargantua and Pantagruel are products of their society, for they are interested in questions of education, politics, war. Thus, they perpetuate the logistics of the discursive, intellectual rhythm which is on the surface of a work of art. Panurge, on the other hand, represents the quest for a sort of education in life, outside societal institutions. The charming rogue wants to have fun, to go on useless voyages, to drink and feast. Not only does he not uphold society's interest, he is outside its limits, defined by society in that he rebels against it. Perhaps Rabelais, tired of ideas, was inadvertently carried along by his creation of Panurge – the "son" of his asocial, emotional self. One might characterize Panurge's activities as irrational, as stylistically circular, while those of the giants are rational, logical, and stylistically linear. Between Panurge and Pantagruel, the interplay of circularity and linearity perpetuates the conflict/resolution rhythm of literary tension.

The giants become progressively human as they concern themselves with human problems. At the same time, Panurge becomes more giant-like as he progressively becomes more and more important in the work. The giants evolve from physical to intellectual beings, while Panurge remains overtly physical and emotional. That Panurge does not arrive at maturity is not astonishing. Given that the unfinished work is Rabelais's immortality, it is appropriate that Panurge as Rabelais's emotional child would also be unfinished. Conversely, one could say that Rabelais's work is an organic totality where everything finishes and begins again at each instant. Panurge starts out as a brave child and ends as a frightened one; everything or nothing is possible for him. This brings up the problem of unity of character.

Panurge, viewed from an emotional perspective, as a child, could be considered both unified and not unified as a character. It has been proposed that mythologies delineate three periods of unity in human development — the dependent child, the responsible adult and the wise older person. At these stages, definite emotional patterns of behavior coincide with physical and intellectual development. However, modern psychology has emphasized the fact that emotional development does not always keep pace with physical and intellectual growth. In the realm of the emotions there is constant flux and change; growth and regression paradoxically take place side by side. For instance, an adult may have the emotional "age" of a child or the wisdom of an older person. Thus, one cannot talk of an emotionally unified age except in very broad terms. Insofar as a child is daily changing physically, emotionally and intellectually, and thereby is constantly in the process of reaching new stages, one must say that he is not unified, if one takes as a given that unity implies a static base. Within this context, neither could one call an adult a unified person, for he is made up of the child he was, the adult he is and his own idea of the older person he will become. To speak of unity of character, then, one must focus on the predominate kind of behavior observed. Throughout Rabelais's books Panurge's behavior is consistently child-like; dependent, irresponsible, spontaneous and self-centered, he is a character unified emotionally as a child.

A unified character is said to be one who evolves, but consistently within a given framework. A "round" character is one who evolves with a certain complexity reminiscent of a real person, while remaining at the same time basically consistent. Given that Panurge does evolve from brave to cowardly, from secure to insecure, all the while retaining the dependency and irresponsibility of a child, one might suggest that he is unified as a "round" character. Yet it is obvious that there is no psychological complexity in Panurge, for as a comic figure he seems to be a caricature of a tormented person. One would probably laugh at the idea of a complex Panurge, saying rather that he is like a child who has decided to play at being brave in order to amuse others and who just as readily discards this role for that of coward in order to elicit still more laughs from his audience. One can only determine that in the context of real life complexity, Panurge is not a "round" character. Then, if there is not the realness of complexity implied in a change from confidence to doubt, from security to insecurity, this leads one to ask if there is actually any evolution of character. From early critics such as Paul Stapfer (*Rabelais: sa personne, son génie, son oeuvre*)[38] to such recent critics as Glauser, Panurge is said to exist in Rabelais's work as nothing more than a pretext to comedy; one of the major reasons given for this view is that they do not see any believable evolution of character in Panurge. In this study, it has been stated, on the contrary, that each change which Panurge undergoes is realistically believable and progressively revelatory of him, if one views him as a child. Within this context, his antics, role-playing, fears and fantasies take on the hue of unified behavior. One might even suggest that he is one of the first characters in French literary history to transcend the popular stereotypes, although he never personally attains the reality of expressing credible inner conflict, which bespeaks psychological complexity.

Implicit in the idea of character evolution is the belief that as one evolves he progresses in psychological development or in learning. For instance, when a child becomes independent and responsible, within the setting of Western societies, he is thought to have progressed. The poet, however, has always known that such a linear view of personal progress

---

38. Stapfer finds that Panurge functions in Rabelais's work as a pretext for comedy: "Si Rabelais nous avait montré Panurge marié et cocu, cette nouvelle mésaventure aurait été, comme toutes les autres, un sujet de pure joie; car, à travers ses fureurs et ses terreurs comiques ce grand moqué est un moquer qui se gausse de tout et de lui-même; Panurge ne prend pas Panurge au sérieux." Paul Stapfer, *Rabelais: sa personne, son génie, son oeuvre* (Paris: Librairie Armand Colin, 1906), p. 398.

is not an absolute and he has even advocated a return to childhood vision and spontaneity as a state superior to that of being a civilized, responsible adult. Despite poetic ideals, Western societies hold for themselves as well as for their individual members the value that becoming civilized indicates progress. In his book, *The Concept of the Primitive,* Ashley Montagu refutes this idea:

> Since we are the latest bearers of human development we reason, therefore, that we are the most fully developed. This rather ortholinear view of development is widely held, and it is, of course, widely believed to be in harmony with the evolutionary facts. The truth is that evolutionary processes do not proceed in straight lines but are more accurately observed to assume a reticulate form. And so it has been in the evolution of man, both physically and culturally. So entrenched, however, have our beliefs become concerning the ortholinear evolution of man that our conceptions of "progress", "development", and "evolution" have rendered the assumption automatic that what developed later in time must therefore be more "advanced" and more "evolved" than that which developed earlier .... Since straight-line evolution is taken for granted by so many, it followed that the more advanced developed from the less advanced, from the "primitive" and that the former was "superior" to the latter.[39]

The primitive has often been compared to the child in terms of his actions and mentality. Jules Henry comments on Kierkegaard's conception of "primitive": "To be primitive means to be unafraid to be oneself; to not fall into the common patterns of existence offered by 'the multitudes of men' ".[40] This point of view suggests the possibility that Panurge's evolution, which is actually revelation of his child-likeness, may be the expression of a state superior to that of civilized adulthood, although it obviously does not tally with the traditional image of progress. At least, Panurge as child-man symbolizes a part of the human being which is important and may be to some degree acceptably retained in everyone, insofar as one can admit to the reality of irrationality and fantasy. Norman O. Brown further relates the primitive to the child, indicating the lack of repression in the two:

> Primitive is that level of culture in which the rhythm of what Freud calls the primary process − the rhythm of dreams and childhood play − is predominant.

---

39. Ashley Montagu, "The Fallacy of the 'Primitive'," pp. 1-6 in *The Concept of the Primitive,* ed., Ashley Montagu (New York: The Free Press, 1968), pp. 1-2.
    40. Jules Henry, "The Term 'Primitive' in Kierkegaard and Heidegger," pp. 212-28 in *The Concept of the Primitive,* ed., Ashley Montagu (New York: The Free Press, 1968), p. 215.

Civilized is that level of culture which effectively represses the rhythm of the primary process in favor of rationality and the reality-principle.[41]

Finally, leaving the idea that unbridled emotional response character-izes the child and the primitive, one can say that from an intellectual point of view, the primitive and the child, free from the subjugations of adult society, become the embodiment of the spirit of Renaissance new thinkers who as cynics and doubters questioned traditional concepts of reason and authority.

One cannot talk about Panurge as child without considering the importance of play and fun in his activities. Since theories on the meaning and purpose of play are myriad, one can only touch on them cursorily. Huizinga says in *Homo Ludens* that the majority of hypothe-ses have one thing in common: they start from the assumption that play must serve something which is not play, that it must have some kind of biological purpose. Most of these theories only deal incidentally with the question of what play is in itself and what it means for the player.[42] In trying to elucidate the nature of play beyond its biological function, Huizinga lists various characteristics. First, play is said to be free.[43] The freedom lies in the fact that play is free from work, free from the "reality-principle" and is rather governed by the "pleasure-principle".[44] For instance, the goal of play is an end in itself; whether one plays to win, to lose, to divert oneself, it is always executed within the confines of the activity's not being "real". The goal of activity in the "real" world, on the contrary, is not an end in itself; one works for wages, for prestige, and so forth, as well as for the intrinsic value of the endeavor. A second attribute of play is that it is voluntary and thus by its very nature spontaneous whereas one must often submit oneself involuntarily to the constraints of work. In that play is freely chosen, one of its goals is to give pleasure, while an implicit goal in work activity is that it be useful to society.[45] A third characteristic of play is that it is limited in time and space. A further narrowing of play within

41. Norman O. Brown, *Life Against Death: The Psychoanalytical Meaning of History* (New York: Random House, Inc., 1959), p. 37.

42. Huizinga, p. 2.

43. Huizinga, p. 8.

44. Huizinga, p. 8.

45. Jean Piaget, *La Formation du symbole chez l'enfant* (Neuchatel: Delachaus & Niestlé S.A., 1945), p. 116.

space provides the subdivision of individual or social, primary or secondary.

Primary games are largely individual and are said to be consciously played by children who are learning motor skills or simply learning to relate to others socially; in Piaget's terms, primary games are a matter of assimilating oneself into the world and accommodating oneself to that world. Secondary games tend to be social and are played on an unconscious, psychological level among members of a group. Panurge's tricks belong to the realm of primary games; he is consciously trying to forge an identity within the world, albeit as a rapscallion. On the level of playing at being a child in relation to Pantagruel and his companions, Panurge's role-playing belongs to the category of secondary games; he is unconsciously trying to gain psychological control in the group. Panurge's primary games (tricks) are individually conceived and executed; he makes use of creative imagination and sets his own rules. On the contrary, the secondary games are social, requiring the participation of others and a set of rules which are not necessarily pre-conceived or verbalized. It has been stated earlier in this chapter that from the moment Panurge decides to marry, he begins to act, to play at being adult; this is a primary game, a conscious effort at a role which will accommodate him to society. His role of child is a secondary game, played unconsciously yet necessarily for this is his natural reaction within a group. In *Le Tiers Livre* and *Le Quart Livre* secondary and primary games intermingle with a kind of double role-playing. Panurge pretends to be adult while remaining emotionally a child. Pantagruel pretends to believe him while treating him as if he were still a child. In *Le Quart Livre* Pantagruel breaks the rules of the secondary game by not playing as Panurge's protecting father; at this point, all games cease. No longer able to deal with the reality of having to fend for himself, Panurge loses control of himself; he cannot play at being trickster, charming child or rebellious adolescent, nor can he maintain the pretense of fitting adult standards. Instead, he is reduced to infancy, to a period preceding interaction with the world in which one lives.

A fourth aspect of play resides in the magic and enchantment which characterizes the creative play of childhood. Aware that he is in a realm totally apart from the adult world, the child is free to become whatever he wishes, bold adventurer, bad witch and so forth. He is free to act out what the adult so often must sublimate in fantasy. Of this attribute of play, Michel Beaujour says:

Enfance n'est pas seulement activité physique et jouissance. Elle est aussi le moment où l'imagination a tous les pouvoirs, et en particulier celui de s'incarner dans les choses et dans un langage en liberté. Pour l'enfance, "l'imaginaire est ce qui tend à devenir réel", plus immédiatement que pour le surréaliste qui a dû se refaire une vision enfantine. Le réel et l'imaginaire appartiennent à l'enfant: tout est à lui, chez lui. Il n'a pas encore rencontré les contradictions extérieures auxquelles les adultes se heurtent, hors du rêve et de la rêverie . . . . L'enfant est-il perdu dans son monde imaginaire, ou bien joue-t-il, pour berner les adultes, la comédie de l'imagination? L'un et l'autre, sans doute.[46]

With Panurge, the reader may imagine himself to be bold conqueror, sexual giant, slayer of monsters or joyful trickster.

A correlative of the magic aspect of play is its secrecy. According to Huizinga:

The exceptional and special position of play is most tellingly illustrated by the fact that it loves to surround itself with an air of secrecy . . . . This temporary abolition of the ordinary world is fully acknowledged in childlife, but it is no less evident in the great ceremonial games of savage societies.[47]

In the citation just given, the child is once again compared to the primitive. As primitive man and child-like human being Panurge seeks out the meanings of Rabelais's secrets, the meanings of the systematized game called adulthood.

Of the fifth characteristic of play which comes from its ego enhancing quality, Huizinga says:

Winning means showing oneself superior in the outcome of a game. Nevertheless, the evidence of this superiority tends to confer upon the winner a semblance of superiority in general. In this respect he wins something more than the game as such. He has won esteem, obtained honour; and this honour and esteem at once accrue to the benefit of the group to which the victor belongs.[48]

Paradoxically, as the child frees himself from adult society through play, he simultaneously learns how to fit into this society by his competitive efforts. Panurge's limitless egotism makes him determined to win, to get attention, at all costs. His tricks must be the most outlandish, his doubts the greatest and his fears without parallel. Rabelais's essential mode of writing uses exaggeration to distort reality and thus to obscure further some undisclosed truth. Panurge as both personification and caricature of a child is an exaggerated human being and thereby a kind of giant; at the same time he is representative of the comic

46. Beaujour, pp. 73-74.
47. Huizinga, p. 12.
48. Huizinga, p. 50.

spirit which distorts real life rhythm and perception. Thus it seems that Panurge is not real and is certainly not to be taken seriously, a situation which leaves him free to reveal hidden truths about Rabelais's view of the world.

A final element of play listed by Huizinga is tension:

> Tension means uncertainty, chanciness; a striving to decide the issue and so end it. The player wants something to "go", to "come off"; he wants to "succeed" by his own exertions . . . . The more play bears the character of competition the more fervent it will be . . . . Though play as such is outside the range of good and bad, the element of tension imparts to it a certain ethical value in so far as it means a testing of the player's prowess; his courage, tenacity, resources and . . . his spiritual powers – his "fairness"; because, despite his ardent desire to win, he must still stick to the rules of the game.[49]

In life there are various possible solutions for eradicating tension, resolving conflict; one may submit to the conflicting situation or he may revolt and so forth:

> Dans le jeu, au contraire, les conflits les plus précis sont transposés de manière à ce que le moi prenne sa revanche, soit par suppression du problème, soit que la solution devienne acceptable . . . . C'est parce que le moi se soumet l'univers entier, dans les conduites du jeu, qu'il se libère des conflits.[50]

Thus, the child, frustrated in real life by the conflict between desire to be obedient to parent and to society and at the same time to be free from both, may in his play world resolve this real tension by creating a new kind of tension wherein the punishments and rewards do not seem so real or so severe; paradoxically, the child plays at the tension of life while escaping it. In the same way, the artist's work is a game through which he simultaneously enters and escapes the real world. The reader, likewise, enters a work, experiences identification with and re-creation of certain tensions in himself, all the while aware that he is escaping real life tensions. Play as well as writing and reading fiction bear a strong resemblance to the conflict/resolution rhythm of life. Finally, it is in part because of real life tensions that one "re-creates" and relates to these activities wherein one can resolve problems from a secure base.

Ultimately, Rabelais's work is a kind of game where there is constant interplay of conflict/resolution; there is no final resolve just as there is no final resolve in life itself. Within the work there is a spiraling circle of games, like the ever widening circles created by a stone thrown

49. Huizinga, pp. 10-11.
50. Piaget, p. 156.

into a lake. Within the largest circle which is the work itself there are the farcical games called tricks, serious games of war, academic games of debate, emotional games of sexual encounter and fantasy games expressed by the bizarre voyage. Like a game, a work of literature is an end in itself. This is especially true for Rabelais in that his work ends where it begins and begins where it ends; from *Pantagruel* through *Le Quart Livre,* there is adventure, comedy and exaggeration.

The circles of games are expressed stylistically as well as thematically: one is led around a never-ending circle in the prologues, in the verbal frenzies of description, through the word lists and through the structures of *Le Tiers Livre* and *Le Quart Livre.* Still, within the seemingly futile circles of the work is a linear concept of progress and enlightenment. In *Gargantua* Rabelais insists that the young giant change the kind of games he plays. Amusing games from which Gargantua learns nothing become a symbol for wasted time, for lack of progress and discrimination and ultimately for futility. Under the tutelage of Ponocrates, Gargantua plays only games that further his education by sharpening his mental powers and developing his physical prowess. Likewise, one purpose for the existence of the gigantic game of Rabelais's work is that one may learn something that might further develop the mind. Appropriately, given the mixture of circular and linear structure, the work is couched in terms of comedy, yet strains of satire and of humanistic wisdom run throughout the work creating a kind of tension which suggests that beneath all the humor there is a great deal of serious matter. Although it may seem paradoxical to talk of serious import within the context of comedy, in a sense, all fiction faces the problem of proving itself to be more than a make-believe game.

As mentioned in chapter II, a popular attitude views play, fantasy and fictional literature as unreal, as not serious. In regards to play, Huizinga refutes this attitude; by extension he is also speaking of fantasy and of fiction:

> The "only-pretending" quality of play betrays a consciousness of the inferiority of play compared with "seriousness" .... Nevertheless .... the consciousness of play being "only a pretend" does not by any means prevent it from proceeding with the utmost seriousness .... Any game can at any time wholly run away with the players. The contrast between play and seriousness is always fluid. The inferiority of play is continually being offset by the corresponding superiority of its seriousness. Play turns to seriousness and seriousness turns to play.[51]

51. Huizinga, p. 8.

An elaboration of this view on play suggests that culture itself arises in the form of play. Huizinga ascribes to the theory that comedy derives from the licentious feast of Dionysius and tragedy from a sacred play or a played rite.[52] And from these rites culture is born. Even those activities which aim at the immediate satisfaction of vital needs, hunting, for example, tend in archaic society to take on the play form.[53] From the perspective that culture itself originates in play, one might say that French Renaissance humanists were playing a game by rebelling against the rules of the larger cultural game:

> If ever an elite fully conscious of its own merits, sought to segregate itself from the vulgar herd and live life as a game of artistic perfection that elite was the circle of choice Renaissance spirits. We must emphasize yet again that play does not exclude seriousness. The spirit of the Renaissance was very far from being frivolous. The game of living in imitation of Antiquity was pursued in holy earnest.[54]

Rabelais as product of Renaissance thinking plays at being a humanist all the while playing at mocking the seriousness with which many Renaissance thinkers approached the game of writing and learning. Underlying all this, the author had to play at playing in order to confuse the traditionalist censors of the day. Given this setting, what could be more fitting than that Rabelais become enamoured of his most playful character, Panurge, who becomes a prototype of Rabelais in that he is raucous and joyous, serious and doubting and is finally spokesman for the spirit of the work.

In concluding this section on play, one should look at Huizinga's conclusion as to what the nature of play is:

> The function of play in the higher forms which concern us here can largely be derived from two basic aspects under which we meet it: as a contest *for* something or a representation *of* something. These two functions can unite in such a way that the game "represents" a contest, or else becomes a contest for the best representation of something. Representation means display .... The child is "making an image" of something different, something more beautiful or more sublime, or more dangerous than what he usually *is*.[55]

Panurge, playing at the game of trying to become an adult, expresses man's emotional quest for acceptance, identity and contentment. In

52. Huizinga, pp. 144-45.
53. Huizinga, p. 46.
54. Huizinga, pp. 180-81.
55. Huizinga, p. 14.

keeping with the heightened sense of life found both in play and in a work of art, Panurge's quest is penetratingly drawn through his symbolic representation of a child playing hard at the game of life. This quality of play which makes life bigger than it is implies a kind of dionysian passion. Of this spirit, Huizinga says: "The intensity of and absorption in play finds no explanation in biological analyses. Yet in this intensity, this absorption, this power of maddening, lies the very essence, the primordial quality of play."[56] Panurge is appropriately cast as a comic character for in both play and laughter ordinary life stands still; likewise, a work of art exists outside the chronological time of real life. Alongside the humdrum march of the clock toward death, play, laughter and art affirm the intrinsic value of the life rhythm which transcends intellectual, societal components and permits readers through the ages to relate to a character such as Panurge.

The joy, intensity and imaginary grandeur found in play depict only the positive side of childhood activity; the necessary counterpart of this delight is the component of fear implicit in the childhood state. Characteristic of Panurge, unified emotionally as a child, are his playfulness and his fearfulness. In chapter I a model was set up, describing tension in terms of conflict/resolution. The tensions which seem to motivate much of Panurge's behavior could be called anxieties. The psychologist, Erik Erikson, describes anxieties as "diffuse states of tension . . . which magnify and even cause the illusion of an outer danger, without pointing to appropriate avenues of defense or mastery."[57] From the amorphous realm of anxiety, fears are born:

> Since his earliest sense of reality was learned by the painful testing of inner and outer goodnesses and badnesses, man remains ready to expect from some enemy force, or event in the outer world that which, in fact, endangers him from within: from his own angry drives, from his own sense of smallness, and from his own split inner world. Thus he is always irrationally ready to fear invasion by vast and vague forces which are other than himself; strangling encirclement by everything that is not safely clarified as allied; and devastating loss of face before all surrounding mocking audiences.[58]

An adult pares and molds his life into whatever form he can best manage. He may sublimate his fears of the unknown and of insecurity through cultural myths, through religious, governmental, educational

56. Huizinga, pp. 2-3.
57. Erikson, pp. 406-07.
58. Erikson, p. 406.

and professional institutions. He may neutralize the fears of anxiety through both love and anger. The child, on the other hand, has not yet developed the intellectual ability of neutralizing fears through understanding, analysis or rationalization. At the same time, because of his physical smallness, the child is economically and emotionally dependent on the adults around him; while this dependence can be gratifying, it can also be frightening, for the child is completely vulnerable to the possibility of rejection and failure. Feelings of fear and inferiority are his demons. Morton characterizes this aspect of childhood:

> The child has little sense of perspective where his fears are concerned. In this respect he is very like primitive man. He fears the strange and unfamiliar because he does not understand it . . . . Everything appears "big" to him as to the primitive mind. He feels weak and puny. He finds little law and less justice in his peculiar world. True, there is a law of the gang and of the horde, but it is unscrupulous, cruel, selfish, often indifferent to the welfare of others. Childhood is "an age without pity".[59]

Thus, lacking the sophisticated methods by which adults cope with their fears, the child tends to fall back on primal mechanisms. In order to win attention from his friends and thus mollify any fear of inferiority, Panurge resorts to sadistic tricks. The existential psychologist Rollo May comments:

> Many a child or adolescent has forced the group to take cognizance of him by destructive behavior; and though he is condemned, at least the community notices him. To be actively hated is almost as good as to be actively liked; it breaks down the utterly unbearable situation of anonymity and aloneness.[60]

Although Panurge is much liked by his group, there does come a point when he is told he must change his child-like behavior and act adult. Tormented by fear of facing the unknowns of adult responsibility, by fear of losing the uniqueness given to an adored child, Panurge copes with this insecurity by constantly asserting a boundless egotism. Morton suggests:

> Great and overpowering egoism, excessive self-sufficiency, and self-assertiveness are only too often a cloak for inner cowardice, an overcompensation for grave defects of character. Frequently . . . the fear complex, like the ass in the fable, clothes itself in the lion-skin of sexuality, and, thus disguised, roars for very security.[61]

59. Morton, p. 107.
60. May, *Love and Will*, p. 31.
61. Morton, p. 111.

From this point of view, Panurge's sexual bravado is just another aspect of his child-like demands for attention. Be it sexual hero, sadistic trickster, troubled doubter or frightened infant, Panurge will adopt any guise as he tries to forge an identity in a chaotic world.

One cannot conclude this section on childhood fears without looking at the part played by rebellion. A rebel, like a child, is outside the normal boundaries of society, is even the antithesis of traditional societal norms. Throughout the history of literature, various myths have incarnated the rebel theme — Adam/God, Prometheus/Zeus, Orestes/his mother, Oedipus/his father. In all these myths the same psychological motif is expressed as is found in twentieth century psychological literature regarding conflict between parent and child.[62] In *Pantagruel* Panurge rebels against university scholars, the Catholic Church, the lady of Paris and so forth. *Le Tiers Livre* continues the story of his rebellion against the institutions of the day. In *Le Quart Livre,* without Pantagruel's acting as supportive father, without representatives of institutions to rebel against, Panurge's fears must be faced in a naked fashion; he can no longer use trickery, egotistical bravado or rebellion to protect himself.

In chapter II the rogue was considered as representative of basic tensions and fantasies surrounding the theme of revolt. Since rebellion as a phenomenon is common in varying degrees in children and adolescents, the comparison between rogue and child can be made. Moreover, the rogue and the child resemble one another on more levels than that of rebelliousness against authority. Vexliard gives this description:

> Le vagabond a souvent été comparé à l'enfant, à l'adolescent par son irresponsabilité au point du vue économique et social. Tout se passe comme si le vagabond, ayant confronté les avantages de la vie adulte avec ses servitudes, ses dangers, ses risques et ses responsabilités, ses engagements, avait "décidé" de ne pas "devenir" grand. L'immaturité recèle en effet une faiblesse des activités, d'inhibition, de contrôle (infériorités biologiques mises à part) l'égocentricité (puérile), une inaptitude à établir des relations affectives avec autrui, conséquence d'un défaut d'identifications positives et négatives (hostilités).[63]

Concurrent with this negative aspect of rebellion, characterized especially by immaturity, is a positive side wherein the child or adolescent seeks the individual freedom requisite to maturity by the very act of

62. Rollo May, *Man's Search for Himself* (New York: The New American Library, Inc., 1967), p. 165.
63. Vexliard, p. 85.

rebellion. Rollo May points out that rebellion is as natural a reaction as are the conflict feelings implicit in it. Most human beings, says May, have a need to struggle toward enlarged self-awareness, maturity, freedom and responsibility; paradoxically, they have at the same time a desire to remain children and cling to the protection of parents or parental substitutes.[64] May continues, saying that it is a psychological truth that:

> the child's opening his eyes, and gaining self awareness, always involves potential conflict with those in power, be they gods or parents. But why is this potential rebellion without which the child would never acquire potentialities for freedom, responsibility, and ethical choice, and the most precious characteristics of man would lie dormant — why is this rebellion to be condemned? [65]

The writer, like the rebelling child, must be free to rebel in a profoundly basic sense if he is to be ultimately creative:

> Every real writer is a rebel . . . . His basic rebellion in this time or any other, is directed at the universe itself, and the universe cannot be undone by history, it remains and it provides the stuff which the artist at once rebukes and celebrates. Every truly creative act is an act of rebellion against the universe and a celebration of the universe because it permits this creative rebellion, that is, the freedom of the artist to act.[66]

In Rabelais's work there is perpetual rebellion. Authoritative pronouncements of the institutions of the day are attacked through satire, the ultimate affront being the motto over the Abbaye de Thélème, "Fais ce que vouldras". In addition to concrete reaction against specifics, there is both metaphysical and psychological rebellion. Panurge puts metaphysical truths into question when he refutes the basic concept of natural law. Panurge's doubts about marriage bring about the need for a psychological reassessment of the economic, emotional, religious foundations of society. It is appropriate that Panurge be the agent of much of Rabelais's questioning rebellion against "the ways of the universe" for to give this role to a child-like character rather than to a scholar is in and of itself a revolt.

Yet if a work of literature is to become classically great, it must transcend its rebellious components; otherwise it would be no more

64. May, *Man's Search for Himself*, p. 166.
65. May, *Man's Search for Himself*, pp. 159-60.
66. Leon Surmelian, *Techniques of Fiction Writing: Measure and Madness* (Garden City, New York: Doubleday and Company, Inc., 1968), p. xvii of the introduction.

interesting or valuable than an ineffectual child trying to break the ropes he simultaneously winds around himself. Rabelais achieves such artistic transcendance by superimposing the form of meaning on the chaos that he has awakened. Simon O. Lesser says that the purpose of artistic form is "to transport us to a world committed to life, to love, to order, to all the values the superego holds dear, and thus to allay that pervasive anxiety which is always with us."[67] In this study one has discussed the various means by which Panurge deals with conflict, thereby possibly revealing some of Rabelais's own conflicts. And while the reader's own feelings and fantasies are aroused by the work of art, they are simultaneously appeased and minimized by the false security of the artificial order of form. Form also works to calm the tensions it creates by the psychological process called projection, which is described by Simon O. Lesser:

> Since objectification necessarily involves the projection of our problems upon others — the fictional characters — and thus enables us to disown unwelcome impulses and concerns, it also contributes to the achievement of another goal of form, the minimization of anxiety.[68]

Talk of minimization of tension by form and through character seems contradictory, however, when applied to Rabelais's work where form is often formlessness and character is pastiche. It becomes feasible to speak of form and character in Rabelais only within the context of a psychologically oriented twentieth century interpretation which above all believes in meaning beneath the surface and form within chaos. Rabelais's work, characterized by the implication of meaning to be sought out, takes on the order of unity if one accepts that this meaning is in terms of human tensions and fantasies rather than in terms of truth revealed through well-constructed plot or well-developed character. Actually, Rabelais's stylistic structure works constantly toward secrecy, toward directing the reader's attention away from complex or profound feelings, toward a caricature of the world, which upon analysis becomes a kind of "black" comedy. Verbal frenzies, nonsense lists of words, reversals of meaning, characterize Rabelais's fiction, possibly announcing his vision of the world as chaotic and absurd. At the same time, such use of language functions to enhance the secrecy suggested by the

67. Simon O. Lesser, *Fiction and the Unconscious* (New York: Random House, Inc., 1962), p. 128.

68. Lesser, p. 151.

idea of the *sustantificque mouelle*. Norman Holland offers a clue as to why Rabelais, attempting to outwit the censors of his day, may have directed the attention of his readers away from naked meaning. When a statement is not linguistically what one would expect, says Holland, it:

> looks like what a psychoanalyst would call displacement. That is our conscious attention shifts (to some degree, at least) from the content of the utterance to its form. Attention, concern, if you will, psychic energy, are taken away from substance and given to language. In terms of our model, such a displacement weakens our involvement with the deeper, fantasy levels, fraught with fear and desire; instead, we concentrate our involvement on the verbal level.[69]

In literature one begins by believing that language is in the world and soon one perceives that it masks the world. Michel Beaujour feels that: "Il est pourtant notre seul instrument pour saisir le monde .... Le mythe des paroles gelées est le mythe de la littérature."[70] In other words, by unmasking the enigmatic Panurge and revealing him as the emotional expression of one's child-like self, the reader can then view him as a necessary mask through which he looks to his private, unmasked self. Insofar as Panurge's dilemma in *Le Tiers Livre* and *Le Quart Livre* is his inability to translate his wishes into action, he seems a cardboard character, a linguistic entity. Yet, he is real to the reader partly because of the function of words in fiction. According to Simon O. Lesser:

> Words in fiction are largely used to create sense impressions – images or pictures .... The impressions, are, however, predominantly visual .... The ultimate language of fiction is sensory and, to a quite astonishing degree, visual.[71]

These visual images awaken memories, dreams and fears in the reader; thus, he knows Panurge.

Finally, there is an important link between the structural forms of *Pantagruel, Le Tiers Livre* and *Le Quart Livre* and Panurge's function in these books. The form of *Pantagruel* is episodic, anecdotal; Panurge is introduced in this book in sketchy lines as the stereotyped rogue, wandering hither and yon, telling tales and little more. The form of *Le Tiers Livre* is circular as is Panurge's quest and as is a child's world. Here, Panurge wanders in a world, foreign to the ordered, linear structure of traditional adult society; Panurge's domain is a world of fantasy and

69. Norman N. Holland, *The Dynamics of Literary Response* (New York: Oxford University Press, 1968), p. 135.

70. Beaujour, p. 140.

71. Lesser, pp. 146-47.

fear, a world of questions without answers, a world where the adult game of compromise has no reality. *Le Quart Livre* is both linear and circular in form. Although Panurge is traveling toward something, the voyage is made in an unreal, fantastic world where traditional value structures have little relevance. This mixture of circular and linear structures, of form and formlessness, of quest with no resolution becomes a refusal of the concept of utopia, an affirmation of human conflict and ultimately a statement of the paradox that is life. Beaujour says:

> C'est seulement en refusant de constituer une nouvelle vérité, c'est-à-dire en se cantonnant dans la contestation et le comique, en se détruisant elle-même à chaque instant, que la littérature peut tenter de sortir du cercle vicieux du langage.[72]

Accompanying Panurge on his linguistic voyage, the reader may transcend the linguistic dilemma by discovering through feeling and fantasy the oldest truth of all, the brotherhood of humanity outside of time and space.

---

72. Beaujour, p. 141.

CHAPTER IV: PANURGE AND PANTAGRUEL

The interpretation of Panurge as a child-like character requires a consideration of how that role relates to his interaction with the other characters and finally of how all the interactions form the mosaic of the work. In the opinion of W. J. Harvey:

> The successful realization of any one character will involve consideration of the aesthetic strength of other characters with whom he is brought into relation . . . . The characters do not develop along single and linear roads of destiny, but are, so to speak, human crossroads. It is within this pattern, this meshing together of individualities, that they preserve their autonomy, yet through our perception of the pattern, their significance extends beyond themselves into a general comment on the world.[1]

This study has characterized the child as someone who is not yet properly socialized, civilized or capable of ultimate recourse to reason. In this context, on an ideal scale, the child would be purely emotional while the adult would be perfectly civilized and rational. Thus, the child is a fitting vantage point from which to consider the emotional rhythm in a work, the rhythm to which a reader relates through fantasy and feeling. Panurge, natural, child-like, portrays the feeling of dissatisfaction with the *status quo* and the concomitant feeling that one has a unique right to express his dissension. The giants, on the other hand, portray an image of rational, social man. When Pantagruel or Gargantua wish to change some facet of their society, they accomplish it within existing institutions such as the educational system and the courts: Panurge expresses his discontent by emotional reactions of rebellion, extravagance and fear. Yet even the intellectual impulse, conveyed by the giants, which leads to questioning and ultimately to systematic doubt, grows out of emotional dissatisfaction.[2] Seen from this perspec-

1. W. J. Harvey, *Character and the Novel* (London: Chatto and Windus, 1965), p. 69.
2. J. F. Rychlak cites Susanne Langer in pointing out that emotions are the basis for reaction and for interaction: "Emotions provide meanings by cultivating a form of rapport among peoples which is preliminary to communication, and there-

tive, Panurge and Pantagruel are inextricably bound together.[3] One might find it useful to look at the relationship between Panurge and Pantagruel in light of the model used by Hegel for explaining dialectic as a method and as a metaconstruct.

According to his model the mind tends to organize life into a triangular concept in which there is thesis (being, consciousness, reason), antithesis (nothingness, the unconscious, emotion) and synthesis (becoming, change, process) where thesis and antithesis are in actuality modified and expressed. Hegel concludes that there is no pure thesis or antithesis, only synthesis constantly playing between the two poles.[4] In the same vein, their is no pure Panurge as child-like character, emotional man, juxtaposed to Pantagruel as pure intellectual, mature man. Rather, the interplay of the couple creates a whole bigger than the two parts which is in the end the work itself, a synthesis, a becoming. One has only to look to Rabelais to be told in literary language the same truth which the philosopher sets up in terms of a scientific model. In *Le Quart Livre* Frère Jan tries to comfort Panurge by telling him that he need not fear drowning since his fate has decreed a death by fire.

fore language is dependent to a certain extent on an emotional community of human beings." Joseph F. Rychlak, *A Philosophy of Science for Personality Theory* (Boston: Houghton, Mifflin Company, 1968), p. 368.

3. In the quest undertaken in search of absolute truth in *Le Tiers Livre*, it is intellectual, rational Pantagruel who tells Panurge that true meaning may actually lie in a realm beyond dialectical logic and beyond rhetoric:

— Mais (dist Pantagruel) il conviendroit que le mut feust sourd de sa naissance, et par consequent mut. Car il n'est mut plus naif que celluy qui oncques ne ouyt.

— Comment (respondit Panurge) l'entendez? Si vray feust que l'homme ne parlast qui n'eust ouy parler, je vous menerois à logicalement inferer une proposition bien abhorrente et paradoxe. Mais laissons là. Vous doncques ne croyez ce qu'escript Herodote des deux enfans guardez dedans une case par le vouloir de Psammetic, roy des AEgyptiens, et nourriz en perpetuelle silence, les quelz après certain temps prononcerent ceste parole: "Becus," laquelle, en langue Phrygienne, signifie pain?

— Rien moins, respondit Pantagruel. C'est abus, dire que ayons languaige naturel. Les languaiges sont par institutions arbitraires et convenences des peuples; les voix (comme disent les dialecticiens), ne signifient naturellement, mais à plaisir . . . . Pourtant, vous fault choisir un mut sourd de nature, affin que ses gestes et signes vous soient naifvement propheticques, non faincts, fardez, ne affectez. Rabelais, *Le Tiers Livre, Oeuvres complètes,* vol. I, ed., Pierre Jourda (Paris: Editions Garnier Frères, 1962), pp. 479-81.

4. Rychlak, p. 287.

Panurge's response is a sort of reprimand to his friend's ignorance of the fact that opposites are not actually so very different:

> A l'aultre, dist Panurge, C'est bien rentré de picques noires. Vertus d'un petit poisson! ne vous ay je assez exposé la transmutation des elemens et le facile symbole qui est entre roust et bouilly, entre bouilly et rousty? [5]

Following the idea that Rabelais hides serious commentary under layers of apparent nonsense, one may impute to Panurge's words, uttered while he is in a state of semi-hysteria, the meaning that if there is any truth to be found about reality, it may lie in an acceptance of what seems to be the irrationality of contradiction. That Rabelais may have intended this message becomes even more possible in light of the fact that a recurrent technique used in the work is paradox. One does not anticipate that giants will act like humans, but here they do; it seems that if Panurge has been roasted alive he will be dead, but he is not; one does not expect that a logical argument can be made for being a debtor, but Panurge succeeds in doing this. These examples show, if nothing else, that for Rabelais paradox is often by its very nature illogical. One might even think that his use of paradox belongs to his irrational side, to his lists of nonsense words, to his scenes of outrageous, farcical humor. However, if one accepts that there is a serious aspect to the work, then Rabelais's use of paradox places him in a philosophical tradition which uses the technique of paradox to provide new ways for looking at old ideas by trying to make rational sense out of a seemingly irrational, illogical world.

In an attempt at elucidating the nature of paradox, A. E. Malloch says that paradoxical arguments "do not exist at all; they are perversions of arguments. But as statements of arguments . . . they do exist . . . . They run counter to expectation or appearance not only in specific subject matter but also as literary form."[6] In subject matter, Rabelais uses paradox specifically to argue, for example, that the most natural, the most "human" people are often irresponsible by the standards of societal laws (*l'éloge paradoxal*); at the extreme, the whole work is a paradox, a quest to answer questions already known to be unanswerable. In form, Rabelais uses paradox as a device for satire; more

---

5. Rabelais, *Le Quart Livre, Oeuvres complètes,* vol. II, ed., Pierre Jourda (Paris: Editions Garnier Frères, 1962), pp. 138-39.

6. A. E. Malloch, "The Techniques and Function of the Renaissance Paradox," in *Studies in Philology,* LIII (Chapel Hill: The University of North Carolina Press, 1956), p. 193.

generally, the form of the work is totally paradoxical in that a serious, philosophical quest is expressed through fantasy and comedy. Thus, Rabelais uses paradox as one might use logic: "Logic operates upon concepts which by definition abstracts from the world of existent things. Paradox controls and makes intelligible this multiple world much as two negative units in algebra, when multiplied, bring forth a positive answer."[7] Paradox becomes Rabelais's *modus operandi* for creating and expressing the synthesis which is the work, neither fragmentary nor whole, yet at the same time both, as is life. Alan Watts describes the difficult task which must be undertaken by a writer who tries to depict paradox: "For thousands of years human history has been a magnificently futile conflict, a wonderfully staged panorama of triumphs and tragedies based on the resolute taboo against admitting that black goes with white."[8]

One of the major paradoxes in Rabelais's work is the fidelity between the seemingly most unlikely characters, Panurge and Pantagruel. Up to this point their attraction has been interpreted as a symbolic union between social man (adult) and natural man (child). Before looking further at the possible meanings and total import of this relationship, it might prove beneficial to examine a concept fundamental to Rabelais's work — the concept of "natural". In E. P. Rieff's interpretation of Freudian theory, the destruction of natural law as a conceptual basis for societal thought led man to the analytic attitude, that is to the realization that he must take upon himself the moral management of his life:

> To reserve the capacity for neutrality between choices even while making them, as required by this new science of moral management, creates a great strain, both intellectually and emotionally. It demands the capacity to entertain multiple perspectives upon oneself and even upon beloved others, and the finesse to shift from one perspective to another, in order to soften the demands upon oneself in all the major situations of life .... Such flexibility is not easily acquired. In fact, the attainment of psychological manhood is more difficult than any of the older versions of maturity precisely because that manhood is no longer protected by any childish fantasy of having arrived at some saving place where meanings reside, like gods in the heavens.[9]

7. Malloch, p. 203.

8. Alan Watts, *The Book: On the Taboo Against Knowing Who You Are* (New York: Pantheon Books, 1966), pp. 46-47.

9. Sigmund Freud, *Early Psychoanalytical Writings,* ed. and intro. (pp. 7-24) Edward P. Rieff (New York: Collier Books, 1963), pp. 13-14.

Suggestive of the analytic attitude, Rabelais asks his readers to assume their own personal moral management, for through the use of exaggeration, satire and paradox he leads his readers to question the accepted "truths" of an old order of values. Rabelais is most likely leading the reader down the paths of his own doubts; at the same time, he is one of the first writers to introduce the analytic procedure of thought which has characterized modern Western thought since the Renaissance era.[10]

Rabelais's analytic quest is an effort to establish his own concept of natural law, physically, emotionally and intellectually. In his search for *le vrai naturel* Rabelais moderates between the work and the reader much as Ponocrates, Gargantua's tutor, directs the change of his pupil from the bad life to the good life:

> Quand Ponocrates congneut la vitieuse maniere de vivre de Gargantua, delibera aultrement le instituer en lettres, mais pour les premiers jours le tolera, considerant que Nature ne endure mutations soubdaines sans grande violence. Pour doncques mieulx son oeuvre commencer, supplia un sçavant medicin de celluy temps, nommé Maistre Theodore, à ce qu'il considerast si possible estoit remettre Gargantua en meilleure voye, lequel le purgea canonicquement avec elebore

10. J. A. C. Brown synthesizes and summarizes the view of history described by Erich Fromm, Burckhardt, Tawney, Max Weber, Brentano, Alfred Martin and Lewis Mumford among others: "In the late Middle Ages . . . the structure of society began to change and with it the personality of the individual. The rise of a new merchant class based upon private capital, competition, and individual enterprise disrupted the static unity of feudalism, and a growing individualism began to make its appearance in other spheres. This process came to a peak at the time of the Renaissance, when a growing individualism was noticeable in all social classes and affected all spheres of human activity, taste, fashion, art, philosophy, and theology. Whereas the builders of the Gothic cathedrals had been content to remain for the most part anonymous, the architect in the new era wished to be known to his public . . . art began to take a new pleasure in the representation of the naked human body, and the pagan philosophers of Greece and Rome once more came to be studied as their books came to be available. The old static society of fixed classes became one in which status was mobile and one could move more or less freely up − and . . . down − the social ladder . . . . The "subjective" side at the same time asserted itself with corresponding emphasis; man became a spiritual "individual" and recognized himself as such. But the new individualism was paralleled by a new despotism, and in gaining freedom and self-awareness emotional security was lost . . . . The individual could no longer depend upon the security of his traditional status and became acutely aware that everything depended upon his own efforts. Freed from the bondage of tradition and fixed status and role, he was also freed from the ties which had given him security and a sense of belonging." J. A. C. Brown, *Freud and the Post-Freudians* (Baltimore: Penguin Books, 1967), p. 160 and pp. 156-58.

de Anticyre et par ce medicament luy nettoya toute l'alteration et perverse habitude du cerveau. Par ce moyen aussi Ponocrates luy feist oublier tout ce qu'il avoit apris soubz ses antiques precepteurs . . . . Pour mieulx ce faire, l'introduisoit es compaignies des gens sçavans que là estoient.[11]

Likewise, Rabelais wants to purge the reader of his old views and habits, but in order not to shock him too severely, he veils his suggestions in comedy, satire, paradox, exaggeration, while asking the reader to "rompre l'os et sugcer la sustantificque mouelle" (*Gargantua,* 7). Disguised as a doctor, Rabelais advises the purgative of alcoholic beverage. The natural goodness of a euphoric state of joy and spontaneity becomes synonymous with drinking. Muir comments on the symbolic significance of drink in Rabelais:

> In Rabelais it is given a moral foundation, and regarded as a rare and precious natural gift out of which the utmost good must be got by civilising it . . . . Panurge, and . . . . Pantagruel are always the better for their drinking.[12]

Another purgative recommended by the good doctor is laughter. Finally, the characters themselves become metaphors of the purge. The giants start out as animals which are made better by becoming civilized and human through Renaissance education. While Gargantua is originally physically dirty, gluttonous and lazy, Panurge is morally dirty; he plays mean, sadistic tricks on other people. Rabelais succeeds in making him somewhat better morally, although he never becomes a type to emulate. That Panurge never arrives at maturity or rationality may be an attempt on the part of Rabelais to say that one must retain some of the daimonic spirit lest he become emotionally uninteresting and even sterile as do the giants after their size is no longer a focal point. In any case, Panurge in his rejection of traditional values and accepted answers, exposes the doubt implicit in man-made answers. In the same manner, a child makes statements and asks questions that adults often ignore; they have partially circumvented the child's uncertainty by creating systems of answers which alleviate doubt and temper insecurity.

The pursuit to elucidate *le vrai naturel* takes many shapes in the work. Panurge appears in the *Pantagruel* speaking many seemingly academic languages which are nonetheless incomprehensible; as a result he does not communicate. When he finally uses his native language, Panur-

11. Rabelais, *Gargantua, Oeuvres complètes,* vol. I, ed., Pierre Jourda (Paris: Editions Garnier Frères, 1962), pp. 87-88.

12. Edwin Muir, "Panurge and Falstaff," pp. 166-181 in *Essays on Literature and Society* (Cambridge: Harvard University Press, 1965), p. 167.

ge is understood, accepted and even warmly welcomed. This is a small lesson, illustrative of the old adage, "Be yourself", be natural. In *Le Tiers Livre* Panurge again tries to communicate a request by using language vastly different from everyday speech. In *l'éloge paradoxal* he speaks a language that is totally comprehensible, yet it is the exquisite lyricism of pure poetry and thus not natural speech. Pantagruel denies him the possibility of becoming a debtor, a state he finds unnatural because it runs counter to societal tradition. However, when Panurge expresses angrily, but in a natural style, his frustration with his new role of responsibility, Pantagruel agrees to give him any assistance possible. Whatever Panurge does or says seems to be acceptable to Pantagruel as long as he behaves in line with his natural bent. Panurge's doubts in face of responsibility or his fear during a raging storm seem to Pantagruel natural reactions and thus acceptable. However, Pantagruel disapproves of the ridiculous garb donned by Panurge in *Le Tiers Livre* as a symbol of frustration. Possibly Rabelais is indicating that honest questions and conflicts are natural and even good while a sophomoric attempt to draw public attention to one's plight is both immature and in bad taste. Another example of Pantagruel's dislike for pretention and artifice is described when he meets the limousin scholar who tries to impress him with his use of scholastic jargon:

> Quelque jour, je ne sçay quand, Pantagruel se pourmenoit après soupper avecques ses compaignons, par la porte dont l'on va à Paris. Là rencontra un escholier tout jolliet qui venoit par icelluy chemin, et, après qu'ilz se furent saluez, luy demanda:
> "Mon amy, d'ont viens tu à ceste heure? "
> L'escholier luy respondit:
> "De l'alme, inclyte, et celebre academie que l'on vocite Lutece."
> — Qu'est ce à dire? dist Pantagruel à un de ses gens.
> — C'est (respondit-il) de Paris.[13]

As the conversation continues, Pantagruel becomes increasingly confused until one of his friends explains to him:

> Seigneur, sans doubte, ce gallant veult contrefaire la langue des Parisians; mais il ne faict que escorcher le latin, et cuide ainsi pindariser, et luy semble bien qu'il est quelque grand orateur en françoys, parce qu'il dedaigne l'usance commun de parler. (*Pantagruel*, 246)

Pantagruel becomes so angry upon learning the truth that he begins to

---

13. Rabelais, *Pantagruel, Oeuvres complètes*, vol. I, ed., Pierre Jourda (Paris: Editions Garnier Frères, 1962), p. 244.

choke the scholar. The poor Limousin lapses into the tongue of his region, at which he is released: "A quoy dist Pantagruel: 'A ceste heure parle tu naturellement.' Et ainsi le laissa" (*Pantagruel,* 247). The lesson drawn from this episode is: "Il fault eviter les motz espaves en pareille diligence que les patrons des navires evitent les rochiers de mer" (*Pantagruel,* 247).

Although Panurge is often portrayed as symbolic of natural man, it is Pantagruel who sets the standards for what is acceptable as natural behavior. Perhaps in this he serves as spokesman for Rabelais's intellectual side, weighing, measuring, rationally deciding just how much irrationality, just how much spontaneous lack of discipline is desirable and finally acceptable. The intellectual process by its very nature shuns and represses the naturalness of ungoverned spontaneity. Yet Rabelais (Pantagruel) feels and sees the need for integration; Pantagruel helps Panurge to become socially acceptable, but not stifled, naturally spontaneous, but not irresponsible. In so doing Pantagruel possibly helps himself to remain intellectual without being pedantic, socially respected without being stuffy. In the relationship, then, each tries to be natural in terms of his own personality; all the while, the intermingling of personalities makes of each a more complete human being.

This study has depicted "natural" man in the image of a child who has not yet been victimized by the rules and repressions of civilized social order, as one whose lack of inhibition and spontaneity make of him a pure emotional being. Michel Beaujour supports this view of Panurge. In Beaujour's estimation Panurge's preoccupation with sex and marriage is another variation on the theme of natural man. According to this critic, the joyous Panurge who gives banquets for the pages, the hilarious trickster, the sexual conquerer, the warden of Salmiguondin who gives away money and property is the image of natural man, the soul of carnival. Beaujour views Panurge's consideration of marriage as the failure of natural man:

> L'homme doit se soumettre à la culture, et remplir ses devoirs. Avec le mariage, la nature s'éloigne de l'homme . . . . Panurge n'est qu'un Caligula manqué. Incapable de haïr la nature ou de se fondre en elle, il doit se soumettre à la société. Sa défaite, son malheur, proviennent de ce qu'il accepte de vivre, et de parler après l'échéance de ses quatorze jours de souveraineté . . . . Le lâche besoin de certitude fait de lui un mort vivant, un survivant. Pour l'achever, il suffisait de le délivrer de ses dettes, en dépit de ses réticences: la souveraineté de la fête, par nature, est fugitive . . . . Déguisé en boutiquier, Panurge revêt aussitôt l'étoffe

emblématique de sa nouvelle condition: le bureau. Il ne lui reste plus qu'à assurer son confort, sa descendance, et l'avenir: faire une fin.[14]

Panurge may symbolize the failure of natural man within Beaujour's framework, but he certainly does not typify the success of social man. What is to be emphasized here is not the success or failure of natural man; rather, Panurge serves as a catalyst to consideration of ideas concerning the concept of "natural". To fall back on a mythical dream of the rebel, the child or the primitive as an absolute image of natural man is a fallacy. No matter what the reasons are which lead cultures to establish traditional order through institutions, there is something quite natural in the regularity and universality of these institutions. At some fluid point of maturity, might it not be a natural thing to attach oneself to one of these societal institutions? Such a consideration leads one to pose the age old questions concerning anarchy versus order, security versus insecurity; each is natural to human emotions.

For Panurge, the idea of marriage creates a feeling of ambivalence about entering the social order at any level; marriage becomes symbolic of ordered society. Pantagruel, on the contrary, is resolute about what steps he will take toward marriage. When Gargantua questions him about his plans for his future, he readily answers:

— Pere très débonnaire (respondit Pantagruel), encores n'y avois je pensé, de tout ce négoce; je m'en deportoys sus votre bonne volunté et paternel commandement. Plus tost prie Dieu estre à voz piedz veu roydde mort en vostre desplaisir que sans vostre plaisir estre veu vif marié. Je n'ay jamais entendu que par loy aulcune, feust sacre, feust prophane et barbare, ayt esté en arbitre des enfans soy marier, non consentans, voulens, et promovens leurs peres, meres et parens prochains. Tous legislateurs ont es enfans ceste liberté tollue, es parens l'ont reservée. (*Le Tiers Livre,* 597)

Marriage, for Panurge, means the end of the naturalness which can only come from the freedom of total uniqueness; for Pantagruel, marriage symbolizes the acceptance of the naturalness of the group rule of cultural law. Beaujour describes marriage as a socially necessary institution:

L'Institution matrimoniale est la cheville ouvrière de toute société: sa forme juridique — et économique — est un microcosme des rapports humains au sein d'une société donnée . . . . Proclamer la légitimité universelle (sacrée et profane) de cette institution, revient à affirmer celle de la classe dominante et de l'ordre

14. Michel Beaujour, *Le Jeu de Rabelais* (Issoudun: Editions de l'Herne, 1969), p. 115.

social. Défendre le mariage, c'est maintenir l'ordre . . . . Pour Gargantua, si le mariage échappe à l'autorité des parents, tout s'écroule: beauté, culture, bonheur, vertu, cohésion du groupe, transmission des richesses.[15]

Rabelais, master of paradox, seeker of the golden mean, cannot permit his readers to feel assured that being married is natural or that, conversely, being unmarried is natural. The ambivalence surrounding the marriage question is structurally enhanced by his placing the quest for resolution between two paradoxes. *L'éloge paradoxal* at the beginning of *Le Tiers Livre* proposes the unnatural state of indebtedness as a natural one; the reader will most likely not accept this argument as valid, but he may be led to question whether the reverse state is necessarily as natural as he might have thought. *Le Tiers Livre* ends with an *éloge* of the marvelous plant, Pantagruelion, a product of nature which paradoxically transcends certain laws of nature because of its strange and wonderful properties. For instance, whereas fire corrodes or destroys all living things, Pantagruelion is not only not harmed, it becomes more beautiful and more useful than before it was placed in a fire. One of the attributes of this plant is that it serves society; it enhances food, turns mill-wheels, helps hidden and inaccessible nations become known to one another, and so forth. Its supernatural powers are such that it almost seems human, for it makes moral judgments sometimes even causing the death of undesirables; paradoxically, the beneficent plant is to be feared by those who live outside the boundaries of societal laws and customs. Thus, one must admit that Pantagruelion is non-plant-like, unnatural. If the laws governing Nature are not irrevocable, what about the laws governing human nature? The reader is once more drawn into Rabelais's circular universe where he is asked to look at a topsy-turvy world.

The search for *le vrai naturel* is reinforced constantly in *Le Quart Livre*. Rabelais's use of realistic nautical terms and language emphasize that the fantastic voyage in quest of "l'oracle de la dive babuc" is only a natural sea trip. The voyagers seem to be a realistic, natural, fixed point in an otherwise exaggerated, unnatural realm where bizarre creatures with unorthodox appearances and manners of living, nonetheless, speak coherently. Rabelais's descriptions of these strange beings serve two important functions for the whole of the work: he is able effectively to satirize existing institutions of his time and simultaneously to

15. Beaujour, pp. 117-18.

present the reader with a gordian knot to unravel by putting him in a situation of intellectual doubt and thereby rendering him emotionally ready to feel uncertain.

The most obvious statement in Rabelais concerning the all-important theme of the quest for *le vrai naturel* is the story of Physis and Anti-Physis which is told at the end of the description of Quaresmeprenant. In chapter xxix the voyagers stop at l'Isle de Tapinois, the kingdom of Quaresmeprenant, a tyrant who is abnormal in appearance and action. He is described thus:

> Les alimens des quelz il se paist sont aubers sallez, casquets, morrions sallez et salades sallées. Dont quelque foys patit une lourde pissechaulde. Ses habillemens sont joyeulx, tant en façon comme en couleur, car il porte gris et froid: rien davant et rien darriere, et les manches de mesmes. (*Le Quart Livre*, 126)

In everything this monster defies what is traditionally considered natural. Frère Jan declares Quaresmeprenant his enemy because he is the antithesis of life and joy. Frère Jan's dislike for Quaresmeprenant reminds Pantagruel of an ancient fable which tells the story of Physis (Nature) and Anti-Physis (enemy of Nature). Physis gave birth to two beautiful, perfect childeren, Beauty and Harmony; out of revenge, Anti-Physis bore two children called Misharmony and Discord. Although the children of Anti-Physis were misshapen physically, morally evil and topsy-turvy in every aspect, their mother praised them and said they were better than Physis's children. Eventually, many people believed Anti-Physis:

> Ainsi, par le tesmoignange et astipulation des bestes brutes, tiroit tous les folz et insensez en sa sentence, et estoit en admiration à toutes gens ecervelez et desguarniz de bon jugement et sens commun. Depuys elle engendra les Matagotz, Cagotz et Papelars; les Maniacles Pistoletz, les Demoniacles Calvins, imposteurs de Geneve; les enraigez Putherbes, Briffaulx, Caphars, Chattemittes, Canibales, et aultres monstres difformes et contrefaicts en despit de Nature. (*Le Quart Livre*, 136-37)

This story is stated in the form of a paradoxical argument thus enhancing the paradoxical idea that what is popularly called natural is often the antithesis. For instance, many people who desire to be powerful are often to be feared, for the very nature of the desire to control and profit from others is potentially a deformation of the goodness in nature. Possibly, Rabelais's fable suggests that those who rise to positions of power are often those who propagate as natural truth views which may be against physical and human nature.

The quest for the most natural and reasonable way to live one's life is expressed metaphorically by the characters. Neither Pantagruel nor Panurge is alone wholly natural nor wholly reasonable, perhaps because it is only in the age of twentieth century psychology that man is viewed as a potential totality. Through the ages preceding the concept of psychological man, the dichotomies were necessary: mind/body, reason/emotion, primitive/social. A tribute to Rabelais's genius is his creation of whole man through the couple, Panurge and Pantagruel. The multiple perspectives which give meaning to this couple equal a kind of kaleidoscopic grandeur which is ultimately the work itself.

First, one will consider the couple as hero and anti-hero, defining hero in a psychological sense, rather than a classical sense, as one who has strength, will and endurance in face of the difficulties encountered in life.[16] Such an understanding of "hero" does away with the formalistic requisites for the super-human classical hero and thus allows a more universal dynamic to which the reader can relate. In broad terms, any person can "re-create" for himself the feeling of having to deal with the conflicts in himself, his society and his age. Thus, one can talk about the heroic element which is potentially in every man. In "Man and Myth" Joseph Campbell refers to the journey of the hero as:

> the pivotal myth that unites the spiritual adventure of ancient heroes with the modern search for meaning. As always, the hero must venture forth from the world of commonsense consciousness into a region of supernatural wonder. There he encounters fabulous forces – demons and angels, dragons and helping spirits. After a fierce battle he wins a decisive victory over the powers of darkness. Then he returns from his mysterious adventure with the gift of knowledge or fire which he bestows on his fellow man.[17]

Rabelais iconoclastically leads his readers to question the external myths of the institutions of his time. Yet he does not say that one must find his own myths within himself. This message, implicit in the work, is for twentieth century readers to decipher or perhaps superimpose.

If one looks at Panurge as an adult, he is obviously an anti-hero, shirking responsibilities, behaving cowardly in face of danger. If, however, one views Panurge's behavior as that characteristic of a child, one might consider him a hero.[18] In *Le Tiers Livre* he accepts the challenge

---

16. Norman N. Holland, *The Dynamics of Literary Response* (New York: Oxford University Press, 1968), p. 346.

17. Joseph Campbell, "Man and Myth," *Psychology Today*, 5, No. 2 (July, 1971), 35.

18. C. G. Jung describes the legendary child hero: "The motif of "smaller than

of trying to learn adult responsibility and of trying to subjugate himself to the implicit conformism. That his response to danger in *Le Quart Livre* is typical of a child does not eradicate the heroic effort of undertaking the quest for psychological manhood. The fantasies portrayed in *Le Quart Livre* are common to the child who must of necessity view the unknown as a chaotic world of darkness with monsters lurking in every corner. Panurge's braggadocio and cowardice are opposite sides of the same coin: he combats the unknown to try to conquer and understand it and thus frightens himself into the retreat of childhood fear. The same Panurge that defeats an army and replaces the head of a decapitated friend is undone by a storm and by the sound of gunshot. In psychological terminology, to conquer darkness is to grow to maturity. Panurge does not achieve the endurance and will which characterize maturity; that kind of strength and calm in face of disaster is left to the obvious hero, Pantagruel. Pantagruel possesses the superhuman resources of the classical hero — physical, intellectual and social superiority. He seems to have no tragic flaw, for in addition to his attributes he unquestioningly accepts the law of family authority; thus, he has few emotional dragons to slay and little need to prove himself. One might, however, turn this statement around and suggest that Pantagruel's tragic flaw is his lack of the frustration and concomitant dynamism which characterize humanity. Panurge, on the contrary, with no family, no money and only ordinary physical strength, must continually search for a niche, must constantly try to prove his worth. Through his alliance with Panurge, Pantagruel not only offers his natural strength, but also adds to his own life a dimension of vicarious excitement. Pantagruel, as a being who has no room for personal growth is in this sense impotent whereas every possibility for personal development is open to Panurge.[19]

small yet bigger than big" complements the impotence of the child by means of its equally miraculous deeds. This paradox is the essence of the hero and runs through his whole destiny like a red thread. He can cope with the greatest perils, yet, in the end, something quite insignificant is his undoing . . . . The hero's main feat is to overcome the monster of darkness: it is the long-hoped-for and expected triumph of consciousness of the unconscious. Day and light are synonyms for consciousness, night and dark for the unconscious." Carl G. Jung and C. Kerényi, *Essay on a Science of Mythology: The Myths of the Divine Child and the Divine Maiden*, trans., R. F. C. Hull (New York: Harper and Row, 1949), p. 86.

19. Jung describes the symbolic significance of the child hero from a psycholog-

Another turn of the kaleidoscope reveals Panurge and Pantagruel in a symbiotic father/son relationship; yet the rapport is quite different from that between Pantagruel and Gargantua. In his role of son, Pantagruel unquestioningly accepts whatever his father's position of authority dictates in matters of education, war, marriage and so forth. In his paternal manner toward Panurge, Pantagruel is for the most part non-authoritarian, acting as companion and counselor, although, on the issue of Panurge's thievery and debts, Pantagruel is stern. Nonetheless, for the most part, Pantagruel is a permissive kind of father while Gargantua is authoritarian, the notable difference centering on the marriage question. While Gargantua chooses the bride and arranges the marriage for his son, Pantagruel allows Panurge to seek his own wife and ultimately to choose not to marry if this suits him better. Yet by allowing Panurge the liberty to form himself, Pantagruel torments his symbolic son. Perhaps Pantagruel is unconsciously trying to keep Panurge dependent on him and thus ever by his side. Or, Pantagruel, as spokesman for Rabelais, does not find in his intellectual wisdom the blueprint for answering questions about emotional conflict and development. Stylistically, the lack of definition keeps the situation open for further literary development.

But, one must ask, why would Pantagruel take over the duty of father figure to someone of his own age, particularly when his personal conception of a father/son relationship is in the realm of what is traditionally considered natural? There is the obvious possibility that Pantagruel is so secure and assured of his place in the world that he can altruistically give of his strength to others in need. At the same time, through a hidden, if not unconscious, contract Pantagruel gains from Panurge a different vision of the world, much as a parent re-experiences a fresh view of the world through the eyes of his children. Muir suggests that:

ical perspective: "The child is born out of the womb of the unconscious, begotten out of the depths of human nature, or rather out of living Nature herself. It is a personification of vital forces quite outside the limited range of our conscious mind; of ways and possibilities of which our one-sided conscious mind knows nothing.... It represents the strongest, the most ineluctable urge in every being, namely the urge to realize itself. It is, as it were, an incarnation of the inability to do otherwise. The urge and compulsion to self-realization is a law of nature and thus of invincible power, even though its effect, at the start, is insignificant and improbable." Jung, pp. 89-90.

In portraying the relations between the kind Prince and Panurge, Rabelais is telling us what he thought was desirable and in certain circumstances possible. Panurge represents a natural potency of human nature which may be treated in two ways; it can be repressed or cast out to follow its own devices, or accepted and assimilated and civilised. In drawing Panurge into the majestic circle of Gargantua and Pantagruel and making him in time an admirable though unconventional member of it, Rabelais acted symbolically in the tradition of what was once the French spirit, which conceived civilisation as an endlessly hospitable thing in which all the variety of human minds has a place.[20]

Insofar as Panurge represents the child-like part of man which may feel overwhelmed by the insecurities and contradictions in life, it is understandable that he would try to escape some of the terror of freedom through recourse to a pattern of semi-authority.

Pushing the thesis of parentage a bit further, one might say that Rabelais as creator of these characters is himself the omnipotent parent. In Pantagruel he has an intellectual son; in Panurge, an emotional son. While he is proud of the way Pantagruel thinks and conducts himself in society, he is equally proud of Panurge who rejects convention. Finally, Rabelais makes of the reader a kind of parent, a judge. In the opinion of Norman Holland: "An author often places his reader in the role of parent and begs his absolution."[21]

Implicit in the questioning of traditional institutions and myths is a kind of rebellion against authority. Possibly, Rabelais's alienation from the all sufficient fatherhood of religious dogma and from the traditionally nurturing support of mother Church, created in him a need to seek a more natural principle of fatherhood. Rebellion in order to escape domination is refutation of both the paternal and maternal principles. Panurge's rebellion is against the patriarchal father, society at large, rather than against his symbolic father, Pantagruel. This suggests another perspective on the couple, that of fraternal rapport. Side by side these two set out to face' the world. In this sense, they are equals, each helping the other at different times and in different ways; they are male mothers. Norman O. Brown describes this kind of relationship:

Fraternity comes into being after the sons are expelled from the family; when they form their own club, in the wilderness, away from home, away from women. The brotherhood is a substitute family, a substitute woman – alma

20. Muir, p. 181.
21. Holland, p. 52.

mater . . . . By rebirth, birth from one's "real" mother is nullified . . . . and a new spiritual mother is found.22

Panurge and Pantagruel choose each other outside the ties of blood and tradition, as spiritually natural brothers:

> The new bond which permits man to feel at one with all men is fundamentally different from that of the submission-bond to father and mother; it is the harmonious bond of brotherhood in which solidarity and human ties are not vitiated by restriction of freedom either emotionally or intellectually. This is the reason why the solution of brotherliness is not one of subjective preference. It is the only one which satisfies the two needs of man: to be closely related and at the same time to be free; to be part of a whole and to be independent.23

Pantagruel, incarnation of Renaissance wisdom, remains aloof, untouched, a character unified in his lack of evolution, a static character. Panurge changes, evolves, yet remains unified for he is continually running in place, seeking but never finding. Yet, the couple combines the major paradoxes in man. Within the spectrum of roles alternately played, hero/anti-hero, father/son, brothers, friends, a variety of unions are possible, given the dispositions of each. Pantagruel is superhuman, Panurge human; the dichotomies are endless: reason, emotion; teacher, student; civilized, primitive; christian, pagan; noble, peasant; rich, poor; intellectual, exponent of the common sense of folk wisdom; scholar, actor; philosopher, comedian; rational, irrational; apollonian, dionysian; wise, mad; reality, pleasure; society, nature; duty, desire; angel, devil; rigid, flexible. Within these dichotomies Pantagruel's role is rather consistently considered superior to Panurge's role in traditional thought of Western society. As scholar, philosopher, rational man, wise man, he is viewed as serious and thus as important. Panurge as actor, comedian, irrational, mad, is at best someone to be taken lightly and is finally to be ignored. Yet, within the context of Freudian thought one cannot say that Pantagruel is superior to Panurge nor vice-versa. One can only say that the most natural man is the one who succeeds in integrating the multiple predispositions which exist in all men. Edward Rieff comments on Freud's assumption:

> that human nature is not so much a hierarchy of high-low, good-bad, as his predecessors in the business of prophecy believed, but more a democracy of

22. Norman Oliver Brown, *Love's Body* (New York: Random House, 1968), pp. 32-33.

23. Erich Fromm, *The Revolution of Hope: Toward a Humanized Technology* (New York: Harper and Row, 1968), p. 70.

opposing predispositions, deposited throughout every nature in roughly equal intensities . . . . A tolerance of ambiguities is the key to what Freud considered the most difficult of all personal accomplishments.[24]

Is this not the lesson to be gleaned from Rabelais's interweaving of philosophy and fantasy, of scholarly pursuit and drunken gaiety? With a turn of the kaleidoscope the concepts of the dichotomies may become interchangeable. He who considers reason to be superior to emotion loses something of the spontaneity of the one who looks first to his feelings. Apollonian consciousness becomes repressed, sublimated dionysian (body) consciousness siphoned through the mind. The philosopher becomes disembodied abstract thought and suddenly looks like the comedian, the grotesque clown. The angel, representative of man tamed, appears neuter, bland, powerless and the devil, a fallen angel, glows forth in proud rebelliousness, in independent self-assertion, ultimately in the flexibility of an urge to growth. And that which appears to be natural and normal becomes distorted and perverse: "The 'normal' 'adjusted' state is too often the abdication of ecstasy, the betrayal of our true potentialities."[25] The quest for wholeness becomes a quest for union. Jung notes:

> It is a remarkable fact that perhaps the majority of cosmogonic gods are of a bisexual nature. The hermaphrodite means nothing less than a union of the strongest and most striking opposites . . . . Notwithstanding its monstrosity, the hermaphrodite has gradually turned into a subduer of conflicts and a bringer of healing, and it acquired this meaning in relatively early phases of civilization.[26]

Ultimately, the quest of the couple is the search for the one lacking ingredient in the work, the search for Eros, for passion, as symbolized in the form of Panurge's search for a suitable wife. In larger terms, the work itself is Rabelais's passion, is Eros. At the end of *Le Cinquième Livre* Panurge and Pantagruel walk forward together toward the same illumination. The couple has become the larger couple of the artist and the work, the reader and the work.

In concluding this chapter, one must look briefly at the symbolic role of the form of the work. As already stated, a major theme in Rabelais is the search for a philosophy of synthesis, of moderation

---

24. Sigmund Freud, *Early Psychoanalytical Writings*, ed., Rieff, pp. 17-18.
25. R. D. Laing, *The Divided Self: An Existential Study in Sanity and Madness* (Baltimore: Penguin Books, 1970), p. 12.
26. Jung, pp. 92-93.

established by opposing extremes. The Pichrocholine war is followed by the tranquility of the Abbaye de Thélème; the storms in *Le Quart Livre* are superceded by calm; Panurge is offset by Pantagruel. The structure of the work repeats the same technique; realism and fantasy follow each other to weave a surrealistic dream in a naturalistic novel; philosophical treatise and bluff interchange constantly; sheer nonsense and seemingly logical paradox are ever present. This all adds up to the creation of a kind of ambiguity wherein perspectives are constantly changing, leaving the reader dizzy and confused. Yet, according to Leslie Fielder, this very ambiguity is a mark of good fiction:

> Ambiguity is the first resource of the serious novelist, tempted like all the rest of us to clichés of simplicity. But to say that the good novel is ambiguous is not to say that it is difficult and confused (this is optional), merely to insist that it is about moral ambiguity and that it cannot betray its theme. I distrust the writer who claims to know black from white, left from right . . . no matter which of the sides he chooses.[27]

Alfred Glauser says that the kind of ambiguity in Rabelais which one could call the negation of composition becomes an agent of creative transformation; everything becomes open and questionable and thus liable to change: "L'oeuvre est telle car elle peut tout accepter dans ses proportions indéfinies."[28] In its circularity, the work is totally open, leaving the characters free to change, the reader free to pose questions; by the same token, the work is enclosed in its own circularity. In the prologue to *Le Quart Livre* the story is told of a magic fox and a magic dog. By its destiny the dog was bound to catch anything that it came across and the fox by its destiny could not be caught or harmed by anything. The problem of what would happen when the dog and fox met was brought to the Gods' council: "La vérité, la fin, l'effect de deux contradictions ensemble feut déclairé impossible en nature" (*Le Quart Livre*, 19). Thus, Jupiter resolved the problem by turning both animals into stone. Rabelais, unable or unwilling to choose between extremes freezes them into the form of a literary work. Thus, the resolution (synthesis) of conflict and doubt (thesis/antithesis) is the statement of contradictions. Panurge's structural role is that of participating in and maintaining the tension and counterpoint between extremes without resolving anything.[29]

27. Leslie A. Fiedler, *No! in Thunder* (Boston: Beacon Press, 1960), p. 15.
28. Alfred Glauser, *Rabelais créateur* (Paris: Editions A.-G. Nizet, 1966), p. 12.
29. Beaujour, p. 112.

CHAPTER V: PANURGE AS COMIC CHARACTER

Panurge as comic character will be viewed from two perspectives: from a direct consideration of his behavior, one will look at him as stock type farcical character; from an abstract point of view he will be treated as representative of a universal source of the comic which exists in the fantasies and defenses of man. At the level of creation of farcical character, Rabelais consciously uses techniques which are contrived to elicit specific responses from the reader, making of Panurge a kind of marionette. As metaphor of a universal comic source, Panurge belongs to the emotional rhythm wherein a reader mimetically extends his daily feelings and fantasies into the realm of fiction. In this context, he transcends his puppet-like quality and runs away from the creator, possibly portraying unconscious feelings and fantasies in the author as well as in the reader.

Throughout the centuries of literary creation and commentary, there have been scores of theories attempting to describe and explain the comic. In the twentieth century these various ideas have been crystallized in two major theories: Henri Bergson's *Le Rire* (1900) and Sigmund Freud's *Der Witz und seine Beziehung zum Unbewussten* (1905). Later critics have extrapolated from and refined these two theories arriving at a "modern" view which sees the comic as a dynamic process with laws and reasons based in physiological and social reality. To understand the mechanism of the comic process, one will look at some essential ideas in Bergsonian and in Freudian theory. In the final analysis, it will be seen that Bergson's theory is a philosophy of the aesthetics of the comic situation, whereas Freud's study of the psychology of laughter emphasizes the source of the comic which is within each individual.

Focusing on the external comic situation which makes one laugh, Bergson sets up two absolutes: first, the laughable does not exist outside the pale of what is strictly human;[1] secondly, laughter can only

---

1. Henri Bergson, *Le Rire: Essai sur la signification du comique* (Paris: Librairie Felix Alcan, 1932), p. 3.

exist when there is an absence of feeling: "L'indifférence est son milieu naturel. Le rire n'a pas de plus grand ennemi que l'émotion."[2] Consequently, one can laugh only when there is "une anesthésie momentanée du coeur."[3] Some involuntary mechanical event occurs to break the mobility of the normal life flow. For example, a man walking down the street slips on a banana peel, falls and the passers-by laugh. The reason for the laughter, says Bergson, is that humans form visual images in their minds of a harmonious life rhythm and when there is dissolution of the continuity of the imagined logic, the individual reacts to the incongruity by laughter.[4] By falling, the man has broken the normal rhythm of walking. Laughter also occurs because one is shocked at a person's having been momentarily transformed into an object; the fallen man does not fit into the pattern of an imagined life rhythm. Bergson states this premise in the form of a law which is for him a general definition of what makes situations comic: "Est comique tout arrangement d'actes et d'événements qui nous donne, insérées l'une dans l'autre, l'illusion de la vie et la sensation nette d'un agencement mécanique."[5] True to his scientific bent, Bergson gives an explanation for his generalized findings; Freud later disagrees with this explanation. Bergson's analysis of the reason man laughs at the mechanical encrusted on the living is·

> Tout le sérieux de la vie lui vient de notre liberté. Les sentiments que nous avons mûris, les passions que nous avons couvées, les actions que nous avons délibérées, arrêtées, exécutées, enfin ce qui vient de nous et ce qui est bien nôtre, voilà ce qui donne à la vie son allure quelquefois dramatique et généralemant grave. Que faudrait-il pour transformer tout cela en comédie? Il faudrait se figurer que la liberté apparente recouvre un jeu de ficelles, et que nous sommes ici-bas, comme dit le poète, ". . . d'humbles marionettes dont le fil est aux mains de la Nécessité."[6]

Thus, it can be seen that Bergson's interpretation of motivation for laughter is philosophical, belonging to the realm of the intellect; Freud's elucidation of the motivation for laughter takes as its basis the physiology of emotional response. Bergson leaves the physical explanation of how laughter occurs to later commentators, saying simply that to defend against the momentary awareness of a lack of individual

2. Bergson, p. 4.
3. Bergson, p. 6.
4. Bergson, p. 40.
5. Bergson, p. 69.
6. Bergson, p. 79.

freedom, society has developed the protection of laughter which simultaneously humiliates the person who has pointed out that freedom is tenuous and conditional and also functions as a seeming corrective to the unwelcome insight:[7] "Son rôle est de corriger la raideur en souplesse, de réadapter chacun à tous, enfin d'arrondir les angles."[8] From this viewpoint, laughter is seen as a kind of necessary revolt on the surface of social life, a somewhat innocuous denial of man's impotence in face of destiny. However, suggests Bergson, laughter may be more than a mild curative measure: "Le philosophe qui en ramasse pour en goûter y trouvera d'ailleurs quelquefois, pour une petite quantité de matière, une certaine dose d'amertume".[9] The task of analyzing the bitter aftertaste is left to Sigmund Freud.

Charles Mauron points out what he considers a major flaw in neo-Bergsonian theories which view laughter only as a social corrective:

> Beaucoup tiennent le rire pour une sorte de jugement social, conventionnel ou collectif plutôt que personnel . . . . Mais la gaieté du tempérament, le regard qui saisit le côté plaisant des choses . . . sont bien des traits individuals.[10]

And Piddington comments that Bergson's elaborate intellectual description of why one laughs is not general enough to explain many laughable situations, for in Piddington's estimation, laughter is a psychophysical reaction which leaves little time for even the most subliminal intellectual judgment.[11] Freud departs from Bergson by stressing the individuality of the laugher rather than the dynamics of the social situation which elicits laughter, and by emphasizing that laughter is not only compatible with emotion, but actually comes from emotion. It is true that Bergson does not completely deny a connection between laughter and emotion for he admits that if sympathy, pity or fear are aroused, one cannot laugh, but he attributes this to the situations's being tragic and then neglects a multitude of other emotions such as disdain, joy, embarrassment and so forth which can readily call forth laughter.

Freud formulated the theory that laughter is generally a response to the physiological patterns of certain emotions that make one feel un-

7. Bergson, pp. 136-37.
8. Bergson, p. 180.
9. Bergson, p. 203.
10. Charles Mauron, *Des Métaphores obsédantes au mythe personnel: Introduction à la psychocritique* (Paris: Librairie José Corti, 1963), p. 9.
11. Ralph Piddington, *The Psychology of Laughter: A Study in Social Adaptation* (New York: Gamut Press, Inc., 1963), pp. 22-23.

comfortable, such as aggression, indiscretion, incongruity. Consequently, much laughter results from the fact that civilized societies require repression and sublimation of both hostile and sexual feelings:

> Since our individual childhood and the childhood of human civilization, our hostile impulses toward our fellow-beings have been subjected to the same restrictions and the same progressive repression as our sexual strivings.[12]

Consequently, there is a psycho-physiological need for individuals as well as for a society as a whole to find some means by which to release repressed hostility and sexuality. The comic has become a socially accepted avenue of such release, a safety valve to discomfort and aggression. Neo-Freudian commentator, Arthur Koestler, ascribes to comedy the emotions of degradation, aggression, superiority and joy, emotions which he calls self-assertive. In the self-assertive emotions, he says, the ego does not transcend itself but is experienced as a self-contained whole.[13] In his elucidation of Freudian theory, Koestler explains that when the self-assertive emotions are aroused, one either feels frustrated by the stress of sexual or aggressive impulses or superior when one perceives an unexpected incongruity; both reactions result in an emotional tension which is liberated by laughter. Nonetheless, Koestler continues, although laughter may be a reaction to and relief from tension, it does not in itself resolve the tension. On the contrary, the tension is "frittered away in an apparently purposeless reflex, in facial grimaces, accompanied by over-exertion of the breathing mechanism and aimless gestures . . . . The sole function of this luxury reflex seems to be the disposal of excitations which have become redundant, which cannot be consummated in any purposeful manner."[14] The tension of laughter ends in an explosion which is generally of two types: the happy laugh of relief at the removal of some anxiety; or the physiological reaction to an aggressive-defensive tendency or impulse.

Panurge has traditionally been treated as farcical character and as pretext to comedy; a Bergsonian view of the comic explains that Panurge is funny because he makes himself and others into objects of ridicule, into mechanical beings. One sees Panurge duping theologians,

12. Sigmund Freud, "Wit and its Relation to the Unconscious," trans and ed. with introduction, Dr. A. A. Brill, pp. 633-803 in *The Basic Writings of Sigmund Freud* (New York: The Modern Library, Random House, Inc., 1938), p. 697.

13. Arthur Koestler, *The Act of Creation* (New York: Dell Publishing Company, Inc., 1967), p. 54.

14. Koestler, pp. 51-52.

scholars and vain ladies, pushing them out of their normal social roles into the realm of cardboard puppets, making them unreal. Freudian theory would say, on the contrary, that cardboard characters are funny because of the realness of the emotions they elicit. In keeping with the thesis of this study which views Panurge as representative of an emotional rhythm in the work which is "re-created" through the reader's feelings and fantasies, one might say that Panurge is funny to the degree that he expresses those emotions attributed to comedy. Certainly, in *Pantagruel* Panurge typifies the so-called self-assertive emotions: he aggressively asserts his God-like will in order to degrade others and then laugh at their plight, thus maintaining his fantasy of child-like omnipotence and his role of amusing some at the expense of others. The reader may laugh defensively, in a denial of identification with Panurge's victims; he may laugh aggressively, albeit unconsciously, as an asocial feeling or fantasy urges him to pay tribute to the fact that an undesirable person has gotten what he deserves; he may laugh from the relief of recognizing that he has not been duped and is thus superior; he may laugh from the tension of embarrassment at some taboo having been broken; finally, he may laugh simply because he is having fun and thus feels good. Through laughter the reader makes Panurge real by granting him the ability to elicit an emotional response. As Panurge becomes insecure, doubting and frightened, he becomes less assertive, less farcical and less funny. That Panurge becomes almost a tragic figure in *Le Tiers Livre* and *Le Quart Livre* will be considered after one looks at him as a comic character.

The use of alcohol permits the same kind of socially acceptable circumvention by which one may express undesirable emotions as does the comic. The hostile or obscene jokester is never punishable by society for he can always reply, "It was just a joke," and by implication neither serious nor real, just as the drunk may apologize for forward or offensive actions by saying, "I didn't mean it. I was drunk." And societies believe and tolerate the rationalizations. In much the same way, one can deny unwelcome implications or insights gleaned from fantasy or fiction by saying, "It's just imagination or it's just a story." Rabelais iconoclastically uses wine and comedy woven into a fictional fantasy to attack the social ills of his day and to expose the universal foibles in man.

In an explanation of how comedy is used to circumvent social tensions, thereby exposing and compensating for man's frailties, Freud delineates three sources of laughter: the joke, the comic and humor. By examining these so-called external sources of laughter, perhaps one can better understand Rabelaisian comedy, and thereby Panurge's role as comic character. The joke, intellectually conceived, intentionally uses language for the purpose of eliciting laughter. It achieves its effect by using some technique dependent on the wit or cleverness of intellect and thereby evades the hearer's ordinary inhibitions, often allowing a sexual or aggressive impulse sudden expression. Given that the medium of the joke is always language, Piddington explains why a verbal indiscretion or twisting of meaning may result in laughter:

> We learn the correct use of language from our social group, and our employment of it throughout our lives is limited by a code of manners as rigid as that which surrounds any of our less important personal relationships. Thus we may say that each word which we use becomes the object of a socially organised affective attitude; in other words, any proposition in regard to the correct use of language is a proposition relating to the social or moral order.[15]

When someone verbally breaks a social taboo, the hearer may laugh from the tension of discomfort and/or from the pleasure of participating in the rebellious jest. Of the many jokes in Rabelais, one of the best known is Panurge's plea to the lady of Paris of whom he has become highly amorous. As the virtuous lady is about to hear her Mass, Panurge says, "Equivocquez sur 'A Beaumont le Viconte' ".[16] Since the lady does not understand this reference, Panurge explains: "C'est (dist il), 'A beau con le vit monte' " (*Pantagruel,* 329). If the reader is not too offended to laugh, his laughter will come from two sources. First, since there is a split second of confusion before his mind clarifies the meaning of the joke, his laughter is a tribute to an equilibrium having been restored. The momentary tension of question and uncertainty is resolved in the intellectual and emotional pleasure and satisfaction of understanding, although this is not necessarily sufficient cause for laughter. The additional element in this case is probably a strong desire on the part of the hearer or reader to relieve the discomfort experienced at hearing a joke, obscene in itself, and even more so because it is expressed in a church. Paradoxically, the tension of discomfort goes hand-in-hand with the pleasure of breaking a social taboo. Panurge has sublimated his sexual desires through verbal channels and at the same time embarrassed the virtuous lady, thus aggressively punishing her for

15. Piddington, p. 100.
16. Rabelais, *Pantagruel, Oeuvres complètes,* vol. I, ed., Pierre Jourda (Paris: Editions Garnier Frères, 1962), p. 329.

her refusal. If the reader laughs, he has permitted himself, through recognition, the same luxury of breaking the social code. One can look to Freud for an explanation:

> Wit permits us to make our enemy ridiculous . . . in other words, wit affords us the means of surmounting restrictions and of opening up otherwise inaccessible pleasure sources . . . . Laughter arises when the sum of psychic energy, formerly used for the occupation of certain psychic channels, has become unutilizable so that it can experience free discharge.[17]

The second source of laughter described by Freud is the comic; while its origin may be linguistic or visual, its effect comes from a sudden conscious perception by the reader or spectator of a disproportion in mental or physical effort, a recognition that the actions or appearance of someone else are immoderate and inappropriate. Whereas the joke calls for an intellectual appreciation of an intentional use of language, the comic comes suddenly and unexpectedly to the reader's or viewer's attention, conveying an image of incongruity. In Rabelais's world the reader is constantly struck by disproportions and incongruities in language, situation and character. Chapter xiv of *Pantagruel* furnishes much material for laughter. Panurge's explanation of how he escaped from being roasted provides an example of the comic conveyed through language. He describes how he fell down as the roasting spit was drawn out of his body: "Vray est que en tirant la broche de mon corps je tumbé à terre près des landiers, et me feist peu de mal la cheute, toutesfoy non grand" (*Pantagruel,* 290-91). One laughs as he suddenly envisions the incongruity expressed by understatement. Speared and roasted like a suckling pig, Panurge should have been dead; however, when Panurge recounts the episode, he dwells on the fact that he fell down although the fall did not really hurt. The same chapter offers another scene which paints an incongruous image through the use of language. Half-roasted, covered with bacon slices, Panurge is trying to flee from the village when more than thirteen hundred and eleven dogs rush at him:

> De premiere venue accoururent droict à moy, sentant l'odeur de ma paillarde chair demy rostie, et me eussent devoré à l'heure si mon bon ange ne m'eust bien inspiré, me enseignant un remede bien oportun contre le mal des dens.
> — Et à quel propous (dist Pantagruel) craignois tu le mal des dens? N'estois tu guery de tes rheumes?
> — Pasques de soles! (respondit Panurge) est il mal de dens plus grand que quand les chiens vous tenent au jambes? (*Pantagruel,* 294)

17. Freud, "Wit and its Relation to the Unconscious," pp. 698 and 733.

Panurge's reaction to his dilemma is incongruous with what one would realistically expect. Rather than describing panic and fear, he inappropriately says that he found a good remedy for the toothache. In Freudian terms, the reader's emotional expectation of logically understanding what he sees or hears is blocked; the result is a supply of emotional energy that must be discharged, consumed — thus the reaction of laughter.

Chapter xix of *Pantagruel* illustrates the comic of situation. Panurge uses silly, farcical tricks to win the debate with the famous English scholar, Thaumaste. Making noises and gestures like small children at play, these two adults appear in a most humorous light. The incongruity between the reader's expectation of what a serious intellectual debate should be and the actuality of the farce portrayed could easily elicit laughter. Finally, to illustrate the comic of character, Panurge himself is funny, in part, because of the incongruity between his image of himself as omnipotent in *Pantagruel* and the incapacity to put his boasts into action which becomes increasingly obvious in *Le Tiers Livre* and *Le Quart Livre.* For example, although he brags at length about his stupendous sexual prowess, when he is sexually rebuffed by the lady of Paris, Panurge runs away for fear of a beating (*Pantagruel,* 331).

As well as being comic himself, Panurge is also an agent of the comic. For instance, one of his practical jokes consists of sewing the alb of a priest onto his gown and shirt. The priest, saying mass before the gentlemen of the court, removes his alb, and unknowingly disrobes himself altogether (*Pantagruel,* 304). There are two probable explanations for the reaction of laughter at this incident. There is such a breach between the attempted seriousness and piousness of the priest and the physical reality of his standing nude in front of a public gathering, that one may well laugh at the disproportion between what is expected and what is. Freud explains the psychological basis of such laughter:

> I believe that we laugh because we compare the motions observed in others with those which we ourselves should produce if we were in their place . . . . The comic found in the mental and psychic attributes of another person is apparently again the result of a comparison between him and my own ego. Thus the object person becomes comic through his inferiority in comparison with my momentary superiority, or his momentary inferiority in comparison with his ordinary superiority.[18]

Secondly, the reader or viewer may laugh in an attempt to relieve the

18. Freud, "Wit and its Relation to the Unconscious," pp. 769 and 772.

tension of discomfort when a sexual taboo is broken (conflict/resolu-
tion). Perhaps also, some small asocial feeling or fantasy is appeased and
laughter is a tribute to the pleasure of participating in the rebellious
jest; of the primitive, asocial side of laughter, Sypher says that laughter
is often an effort to adjust our repulsion from and our attraction to a
situation.[19]

Before talking about Freud's third source of laughter, it might prove
helpful to examine more closely the nature of laughter itself. Arthur
Koestler clarifies Freud's idea of what happens to a person physiologically when he laughs. One hears words or perceives a situation or event
in two habitually incompatible associative contexts. For example, one
envisions a nude priest saying mass. This incongruity causes an abrupt
transfer of the train of thought from one matrix to another governed
by a different logic or "rule of the game". The reader or viewer does
not have time to make a logical jump from one context to the other;
the result is laughter.[20] Koestler describes the physiological process
that takes place:

> Two matrices are bisociated in the spectator's mind; and while his intellect is
> capable of swiftly oscillating from one matrix to the other and back, his emo-
> tions are incapable of following these acrobatic turns; they are spilled into the
> gutters of laughter as soup is spilled on a rocking ship. What these metaphors are
> meant to convey is that the aggressive-defensive class of emotions has greater
> inertia, persistence, or mass momentum than reason. In other words, thought
> belongs to brain cells; emotion combines thought, (memory) and physiological
> reactions . . . more bodily systems are used . . . . If we could change our moods
> as quickly as we jump from one thought to another we would be acrobats of the
> emotion . . . . Thinking in its physiological aspect, is based on electro-chemical
> activities in the cerebral cortex and related regions of the brain, involving energy
> transactions which are minute compared to the massive glandular, visceral, and
> muscular changes that occur when emotions are aroused.[21]

When the reader envisions the priest disrobed before the gentlemen of
the court, he does not take time to think that the situation is the work
of a fictional prankster and thus very unlikely in everyday life; rather,
his ego says, that could be (is) you, so laugh because you feel embarrassed and uncomfortable. Or when the reader understands the pun on

19. Wylie Sypher, "The Meanings of Comedy," pp. 193-255 in *Comedy*, ed.,
Wylie Sypher (Garden City, New York: Doubleday and Company, Inc., 1956), p.
202.

20. Koestler, p. 95.

21. Koestler, pp. 56-57.

"A Beaumont le Viconte", he does not stop to analyze the fact that words have been inverted for the purpose of creating a sexual indiscretion which is supposed to embarrass him. Rather, he laughs to relieve his discomfort and to attest to the intellectual pleasure of understanding the joke.

Finally, the third source of laughter, according to Freud, is humor. Humor is a philosophical stance chosen by the author who acts as a kind of parental figure, assuring his readers (child) that a seeming tragedy is not really terrible after all. Humor occurs when one expects to suffer or to see someone suffer at the hands of reality but instead the situation loses its gravity. In other words, one sees someone in a situation which one expects will produce anger, pain, fright or despair, but the emotional expectancy of the onlooker is disappointed when the other person expresses no emotion, but, rather, makes a jest. The painful emotion has been detonated and the onlooker can smile or laugh in relief.[22] The humorist has acquired a kind of superiority by assuming the role of adult, even the role of father, while he reduces others to the position of children.[23]

The comic, with its sudden exposure of something funny and the joke as source of immediate intellectual gratification and verbal outlet for aggressive impulses, are created consciously by the author for the reader's benefit. Koestler observes:

> There is an obvious contrast between the emotive reactions of creator and consumer: the person who invents the joke or comic idea seldom laughs in the process. The creative stress under which he labours is not of the same kind as the emotions aroused in the audience. He is engaged in an intellectual exercise, a feat of mental acrobatics; even if motivated by sheer venom it must be distilled and sublimated. Once he has hit on the idea and worked out the logical structure, the basic pattern of the joke, he uses his tricks of the trade – suspense, emphasis, implication – to work up the audience's emotions; and to make these explode in laughter when he springs his surprise-effect on them.[24]

Humor, on the other hand, is a comic pose that the author may consciously adapt as his own filter for viewing the world and as a defense for coping with that world. Freud tries to analyze what would motivate one to choose to be a humorist:

22. Norman N. Holland, *The Dynamics of Literary Response* (New York: Oxford University Press, 1968), pp. 284-88.

23. Sigmund Freud, "Humour," pp. 215-221 in *Collected Papers,* ed., James Strachey, V (Toronto: Clarke, Irwin and Company, Ltd., 1950), p. 218.

24. Koestler, p. 93.

We ask ourselves what makes the humorist arrogate to himself this role? Here we must recall the other, perhaps the original and more important, situation in humour, in which a man adopts a humorous attitude towards himself in order to ward off possible suffering. Is there any sense in saying that someone is treating himself like a child and is at the same time playing the part of the superior adult in relation to the child? [25]

Dr. Rabelais, as humorist, poses as the all-knowing doctor, the omnipotent father, who prescribes not only for himself, but for his characters and readers as well the medication of humor. Humor is in this instance a philosophical pose, a conscious effort at avoiding pain, a methodology of survival; and it elicits a tired, sympathetic smile rather than raucous or joyous laughter. In Freud's opinion:

Like wit and the comic, humour has in it a liberating element. But it also has something fine and elevating, which is lacking in the other two ways of deriving pleasure from intellectual activity. Obviously, what is fine about it is the triumph of narcissism, the ego's victorious assertion of its own invulnerability. It refuses to be hurt by the arrows of reality or to be compelled to suffer. It insists that it is impervious to wounds dealt by the outside world, in fact, that these are merely occasions affording it pleasure . . . . Humour is not resigned; it is rebellious. It signifies the triumph not only of the ego, but also of the pleasure principle, which is strong enough to assert itself here in the face of the adverse real circumstances.[26]

Once again, Rabelais states in literary language what Freud clinically describes. In the prologue to the *Quart Livre* the good doctor recommends "pantagruelisme" to his readers: "Je suys, moiennant un peu de Pantagruelisme (vous entendez que c'est certaine gayeté d'esprit conficte en mespris des choses fortuites, sain et degourt; prest à boire, si voulez.)"[27] Pantagruel, as spokesman for Rabelais the humorist, smiles sympathetically at Panurge, the rebellious, pleasure-seeking child who asserts himself over and over against the vicissitudes of life. And the reader too becomes a child guided by the humoristic wisdom of the artist.

Rabelais's characters are exaggerated, caricatures, in some way out of step with societal norms. There are giants with superhuman appetites and brains who impersonate philosopher kings. There is Frère Jan, a defrocked priest in spirit if not in fact. Panurge, mischievous rebel,

---

25. Freud, "Humour," pp. 218-19.
26. Freud, "Humour," pp. 216-17.
27. Rabelais, *Le Quart Livre, Oeuvres complètes,* vol. II, ed., Pierre Jourda (Paris: Editions Garnier Frères, 1962), pp. 11-12.

impersonates in turn a roguish child and a bourgeois merchant. Misshapen people of all sorts in *Le Quart Livre* impersonate in language and custom the kinds of persons whom societies find normal. Everyone and everything is incongruous with the reader's emotional expectations of normalcy; he reacts viscerally by laughing in order to deny and to correct the emotional tension created by the illogical, incongruous images conveyed.

As a character in his own right, Panurge embodies the spirit of farce; stylistically, he functions as an agent of farcical humor. *Webster's New World Dictionary* defines farce as: "stuffing, to fill in; hence farce: so called because early farces were used to fill in the interludes between parts of a play, (1) an exaggerated comedy based on broadly humorous situations; play intended only to be funny; something absurd or ridiculous."[28] Farce, as one kind of comic humor, is a genre which usually treats the most primitive basic instincts such as sadism, aggression and sex. These instincts are said to represent man's animal nature, his response at the level of physiology, and thus are the lowest common denominator of human feelings and fantasy. Farcical characters are commonly stigmatized as types, rather than as unique individuals. Farcical humor, existing at the most basic physiological level, does not allow for the intellectual, emotional complexity portrayed by "round" characters. Looking only at Panurge's farcical behavior, one would call him a most uncomplicated character. Yet there is a perspective from which farcical Panurge attains a certain complexity and thus transcends the flatness of type. If one views his farcical nature as symbolic of asocial feelings and fantasies that are basic to human nature and that depend on the safety of a vicarious outlet, then Panurge as farcical character becomes a part of the complex system of emotional response that links man to man regardless of time and place. It is at the level of sexual farce that a reader from the Western world, with its traditionally repressive sexual mores, will must likely laugh aloud at Rabelais. Koestler remarks: "Primitive jokes arouse crude, aggressive or sexual emotions by means of a minimum of ingenuity."[29] It is this aspect of Rabelais's work which has incurred such critical disapproval through the centuries. Likewise this facet of Rabelaisian humor has caused some

28. *Webster's New World Dictionary of the American Language* (New York: The World Publishing Company, 1960), p. 526.

29. Koestler, p. 87.

critics to suggest that there is little art in Rabelais. In defense of Rabelais, one might consider the problem from a different perspective. Insofar as his is a comic art, designed to purge the reader through laughter, one cannot castigate him for achieving his goal, no matter what the means. His farcical humor is the essence of the raucous, rebellious spirit which is so complementary to his display of extensive scholastic learning. Yet, if one must make hierarchical evaluations, one might say that farce is Rabelais's low level of art, while the all-pervasive satire is the other extreme. Satire is intellectually conceived and understood and is thereby readily acceptable to critics and scholars while bawdy sexual humor touches on an emotional core which is only loosely attached to the intellect — the animal part of human nature which belongs to bum and scholar alike, and which is, thus, easily denied or rejected by the intellect. Sypher says that when one is in the presence of a sexual indiscretion:

> There we drop the mask which we have composed into the features of our decent, cautious selves. Rabelais strips man of his breeches; he is the moral "sans-culotte". Psychologists tell us that any group of men and women, no matter how "refined", will, sooner or later, laugh at a "dirty" joke, the question being not whether they will laugh but when, or at precisely what "dirty" joke; that is, under exactly what co-efficient of stress a code of "decency" breaks apart and allows the human being to fall steeply down to the recognition of his inalienable flesh.[30]

In reaction to Rabelais, a reader may laugh a great deal because of the many sexual references: obscene words, vulgar jokes, praise of the male genitalia, discourses on wiping oneself. Panurge in *Pantagruel* represents the spirit of sexual freedom, a rebellious insistence on the goodness and naturalness of physical reality. If one laughs at Panurge's lack of sexual inhibition, he laughs not only from his own embarrassed discomfort, but also from the pleasure of participating in Panurge's spontaneous glee. The reader has to some degree returned to his own childhood, a period when the societal dicta of "right" and "wrong" have no meaning. As representative of natural man, Panurge knows nothing of the civilized amenities that go into wooing a woman. In a Tarzan-like manner he approaches one of the great ladies of Paris: "— Par Dieu, (dist il), si veulx bien moy de vous, mais c'est chose qui ne vous coustera rien, et n'en aurez rien moins. Tenez, (montrant sa longue braguette), voicy Maistre Jan Chouart qui demande logis" (*Pantagruel,* 331). The civilized

30. Sypher, "The Meanings of Comedy," p. 208.

reader must break through his social armor, his historical being, to the leveling human factor of physical necessity: laughter is his admission that he is civilized and thus a bit uncomfortable at the breaking of social taboos and simultaneously his admission that he is also natural man. Enck explains:

> Sex is a sphere peculiarly rich in comic possibilities precisely because of its sacred nature, its size as a social fact, and the intense personal relationship it involves. A special comic possibility in the sex relation comes from the contradiction between man as a natural creature and man as a historical person.[31]

Of course, the depth of one's laughter must be dependent on the degree to which open statements about sexual functions are natural or unnatural to a given age and society and finally to a particular individual:

> The contrast upon which the ludicrous quality [which elicits laughter] depends is not, as Bergson would have us believe, between the living and the inanimate, but between that which conforms to current social norms and that which does not.[32]

Most of Panurge's sexual transgressions are verbal and thus often combine the vulgarity of farce with the intellectuality of wit. Panurge's explanation of how one might rebuild the walls of Paris ends up with a purely vulgar tale about the manner in which a fox kept an old woman's genital area free from flies (*Pantagruel*, 297-98). However, in chapter xvi of *Pantagruel* intellectual cleverness accompanies farcical vulgarity:

> Et le monde demandoit pourquoy est ce que ces fratres avoyent le couille si longue. Ledict Panurge soulut très bien le probleme, disant: "Ce que faict les aureilles des asnes si grandes, ce est parce que leurs meres ne leur mettoyent point de beguin en la teste: comme dit *De Alliaco* en ses *Suppositions*. A pareille raison, ce que faict la couille des pauvres beatz peres, c'est qu'ilz ne portent poinct de chausses foncées, et leur pauvre membre s'estend en liberté à bride avallée, et leur va ainsi triballant sur les genoulx, comme font les patenostres aux femmes. Mais la cause pourquoy ilz l'avoyent gros à l'equipollent, c'est que en ce triballement les humeurs du corps descendent audict membre: car, selon les legistes, agitation et motion continuelle est cause d'attraction. (*Pantagruel*, 304-05)

This information rendered in academic style is full of potential for eliciting laughter. At the farcical level, the subject breaks the code of public sexual decency by its explicitness and by focusing on priests,

---

31. John J. Enck, E. Forter and A. Whitley, eds., *The Comic in Theory and Practice* (New York: Appleton-Century-Crofts, Inc., 1960), p. 111.
32. Piddington, p. 35.

supposed champions of celibacy. In addition, there is an unexpected and ridiculous comparison of the genitals of priests to the ears of asses. Finally, Panurge gives intellectual validation to his theory by citing both a philosophical and a legal opinion, thus emphasizing the incongruity between the rather vulgar subject and the academic thesis given as explanation. It is interesting to note that this episode is in a sense the antithesis of Panurge's debate with Thaumaste, where the comedy comes from treating a supposedly serious matter in a farcical manner; here an irrelevant and silly question is posed as a generalized statement of fact and the answer given with the utmost academic seriousness.

In a more specifically literary definition of farce, Eric Bentley says that farce embodies the repressed wishes of the majority of mankind "to damage the family, to desecrate the household gods".[33] In other words, Bentley speaks of that part of man which is asocial, rebellious, which strains for freedom from authority, at the same time as one embraces the security of authority. Bentley continues: "Like dreams, farces show the disguised fulfillment of repressed wishes. That is a Freudian formula, but not, surely, one that only Freudians can accept."[34] Farce is a kind of comedy which disguises the least thoroughly the fact that there is something of the destructive orgy in comedy. Paradoxically, says Bentley, the function of orgies is one of a safety valve as well as of destruction. Farce, like the festal carnival, permits an outlet for repression and frustrations in the society so that society's traditions may remain intact.[35] Pantagruel has been described as upholder of the tenets of society and tradition and Panurge as one who refutes and breaks down these same tenets. Expressive of *l'esprit gaulois*, Panurge's humor is primitive, physical and often crude, in other words, farcical.

Chapter xvi of *Pantagruel* describes Panurge's aggressive sadistic sense of humor. He finds great fun in beating pages who are carrying wine to their master. He throws grape-juice in the eyes of passers-by and tosses burrs at the gowns and hats of the good men of the city. It delights him to fasten together people in a crowd with hooks and buckles so that when they pull apart their clothes will tear. As already

33. Eric Bentley, "The Psychology of Farce," pp. 540-53 in *The Genius of the French Theatre*, ed. and intro., Albert Bermel (New York: The New American Library of World Literature, Inc., 1961), p. 543.

34. Bentley, p. 543.

35. Bentley, p. 547.

mentioned, there is a sexual overtone to much of his aggression; thus, he sometimes makes horns in the shape of a male member and places them on the back of women's hoods. The reader may laugh at these sadistic tricks in order to relieve the tension of social discomfort; to release any repressed feeling or fantasy of hostility and sexuality ("desecrate the household gods"); to register his superiority in the safety of a fictional world; to participate in the pure joy of fun-making. And the reader is not socially castigated for laughing because these tricks are ultimately harmless and the victims relatively unscathed.

The uncivilized child is often comic for the same reasons as a farcical character: sexual exhibitionism, destructive behavior which draws attention to himself, repetition of vulgar words as assertive rebellion, characterize the asocial being that one calls child. Bentley supports the comparison between the asocial aspect of childhood and the farcical character:

> Farce . . . while it begins by accepting the bland, placid, imposing facade of life, proceeds to become farcical by knocking the facade down. The farceur, like the lunatic and the unruly child, flies in the face of decorum . . . . It is the impishness, the quasi innocence, the complication of aggression with bizarre fantasy . . . . The dynamic of farce proper derives from the interplay between the mask (of actuality) and the real face (of primitive instinct).[36]

Like a little boy who mercilessly teases little girls in order to get their attention, Panurge fills small cones with fleas and lice which he attaches with reeds to the collars of the sweetest young girls he can find, especially those whom he finds in church (*Pantagruel,* 303). And the buffoon hero of farcical literature is related not only to the asocial child and to the primitive, but is also first cousin to the rogue, the major difference being that the buffoon deals with everything through foolery and jest while the rogue has a few more tricks in his bag. Panurge is a perfect combination of rogue and buffoon — sometimes fending for himself sadistically and other times joking his way in and out of situations. Susanne Langer characterizes the buffoon as:

> the indomitable living creature fending for itself, tumbling and stumbling . . . from one situation into another. He is the personified "élan vital", his chance adventures and misadventures without much plot, though often with bizarre complications, his absurd expectations and disappointments, in fact his whole improvised existence has the rhythm of primitive, savage, if not animalian life, coping with a world that is forever taking new uncalculated turns, frustrating,

36. Bentley, pp. 548-50.

but exciting. He is neither a good man nor a bad one, but is genuinely amoral —
now triumphant, now worsted and rueful, but in his ruefulness and dismay he is
funny, because his energy is really unimpaired and each failure prepares the
situation for a new fantastic move.[37]

Thus, Panurge is roasted alive by the Turks and survives beautifully; he
plays a monumental joke on enemy soldiers and defeats thousands
single-handedly. For the reader he becomes the personified spirit of
rebellion, the desecrator of household gods, champion of the eternal
life spark.

One might also consider Panurge as farcical character from a stylistic
point of view. In the article "Farce as Method" Robert C. Stevenson
proposes that the only essential items for farce are that it be short and
that it use language in a certain way. In farce, says Stevenson, language
must show: brevity, incongruous juxtapositions, mechanical tricks to
catch the spectator or reader by surprise, antithesis of persons, accents
and dialects, staccato succession in speech, action and scene, successive
key phrases, arithmetical crescendoes, exaggerations of all kinds, simple
conduct of behavior refined to its extreme, brutal directness, brisk
reversals, impudent last word.[38] This list of farcical ingredients is almost a formula for the creation of Panurge's behavior. First, the episodes in which he appears are brief and interspersed among chapters of
satire and of catalogued learning. Secondly, throughout Rabelais's
books, Panurge is the constant companion of Pantagruel, to whom he is
antithetical in appearance and character. One can only laugh at the
image of this odd couple. Panurge, "de stature moyenne, ny trop grand,
ny trop petit" (*Pantagruel,* 300) juxtaposed to Pantagruel who, "estant
encores au berseau, feist cas bien espouventables . . . . A chascun de ses
repas il humoit le laict de quatre mille six cens vaches" (*Pantagruel,*
235). Another source of farcical humor is the unexpected juxtapositions in Panurge's speech. In *Le Tiers Livre* Pantagruel asks his companion if he thinks that the codpiece is the principal piece of military
harness. At first, Panurge's answer seems like the learned response of
one versed in philosophy, history, theology, biology and oratory. However, when he begins to mix up Biblical history with manmade history

37. Susanne K. Langer, *Feeling and Form: A Theory of Art* (New York: Charles
Scribner's Sons, 1953), p. 342.
38. Robert C. Stevenson, "Farce as Method," pp. 85-93 in *The Tulane Drama
Review,* ed., Robert W. Corrigan, V, No. 2 (Dec., 1960), 89-91.

and to juxtapose learned statements with "vulgarities", the whole discourse enters the realm of farcical humor. He starts off by saying that he is sure that the principal piece of military harness is not spurs, as is traditionally thought but the codpiece:

> — Je le maintiens, respondit Panurge: et non à tord je le maintiens. Voyez comment nature voulent les plantes, arbres, arbrisseaulx, herbes, et zoophytes, une fois par elle créez, perpetuer et durer en toute succession de temps, sans jamais deperir les especes, encores que les individuz perissent, curieusement arma leurs germes et semences, es quelles consiste icelle perpetuité, et les a muniz et couvers par admirable industrie de gousses, vagines, testz ... qui leurs sont comme belles et fortes braguettes naturelles .... Advenent la multiplication de malice entre les humains en succession de l'aage de fer, et regne de Juppiter, la terre commença à produire orties, chardons, espines, et telle autre maniere de rebellion contre l'homme entre les vegetables; d'autre part, presque tous animaulx ... se emanciperent de luy .... L'homme adoncques, voulent sa premiere jouissance maintenir et sa premiere domination continuer ... eut necessité soy armer de nouveau ....
> — Considerez (dist Panurge) comment nature l'inspira soy armer, et quelle partie de son corps il commença premier armer. Ce feut (par la vertu Dieu), la couille.

Suddenly, Panurge breaks into his intellectual oratory with an unexpected refrain probably from a popular poem or song:

> Et le bon messer Priapus,
> Quand eut faict, ne la pria plus.

Then, he continues his rhetorical expose, looking to the Bible for intellectual validation of his theory about the importance of the codpiece. The reader can only laugh when he perceives the inappropriate juxtaposition of Biblical reference and the vulgar description of Lorraine ballocks:

> Ainsi nous le tesmoigne le capitaine et philosophe hebrieu Moses, affermant qu'il se arma d'une brave et gualante braguette, faicte par moult belle invention de feuilles de figuier .... Exceptez moy les horrificques couilles de Lorraine, les quelles à bride avalée descendent au fond des chausses, abhorrent le mannoir des braguettes haultaines, et sont hors toute methode: tesmoing Viardiere le noble Valentin, lequel un premier jour de may, pour plus guorgias estre, je trouvay à Nancy, descrotant ses couilles extendues sus une table, comme une cappe à l'hespaignole. Doncques ne fauldra dorenavant dire, qui ne vouldra improprement parler, quand on envoyra le franc taulpin en guerre,

Panurge ends his discourse with a joke, a play on words, thus appealing to intellectual as well as emotional sources of laughter:

> Saulve, Tevot, le pot au vin,
> c'est le cruon. Il faut dire,

> Saulve, Tevot, le pot au laict,
> ce sont les couilles: de par tous les diables d'enfer.[39]

A third farcical device listed by Stevenson is the use of mechanical tricks to catch the reader by surprise. A mechanical trick is a kind of practical joke which intends to shock the victim thereby rendering him inferior and consequently laughable. To achieve this effect, however, the trick must be carefully planned and prepared in advance. Panurge is a master in the art of the practical joke. Whether he is shaking euphorbium under the noses of beautiful ladies, thus causing them to sneeze for hours, or using his charm and craftiness to buy a sheep so that he may ultimately surprise the merchant into drowning, the reader learns to expect the unexpected from Panurge. If the reader laughs at Panurge's sadistic tricks, there could probably be found in that laughter a sense of relief at not having been duped – the victim is ridiculous and the reader's ego protects him by saying, be glad that you have not been duped. The reader might also laugh in a kind of aggressive affront to Panurge himself; shocked at his sadism, his lack of feeling, the reader denies him the right to be taken seriously (makes him into an object) thus nullifying any but the most unconscious identification with him. Finally, one may experience the rebellious glee of vicariously participating in an asocial, child-like act.

The farcical ingredients of staccato succession, successive key phrases and arithmetical crescendoes, characterize two of the major episodes in which Panurge appears. In chapter ix of *Le Tiers Livre,* Panurge consults Pantagruel as to whether he should marry or not. The ensuing discussion augments through the repetition of key phrases. Pantagruel advises Panurge to marry to which Panurge replies "Voir mais . . ." and Pantagruel rejoins "Poinct doncques ne vous mariez." Panurge's immediate response is another "Mais si . . ." and Pantagruel's rebuttal is "Mariez-vous doncq". This pattern is reiterated until a compromise measure is found, a quest decided upon. In *Le Quart Livre* (p. 53) the repetition technique is used in Panurge's bargaining with Dindenault. Dindenault's comments are eloquent descriptions of why his sheep are too valuable to sell to someone as inferior as Panurge, and Panurge's unvaried replies are staccato jabs of "Vendez m'en un . . .". The negotiation continues in this vein until the sheep merchant capitu-

---

39. Rabelais, *Le Tiers Livre, Oeuvres complètes,* vol. I, ed., Pierre Jourda (Paris: Editions Garnier Frères, 1962), pp. 433-35.

lates, thus ending the repartée. The reader expects either logical discussion or change of response; instead, he hears repeated phrases that become more ridiculous with each recurrence. The content of these two discussions becomes obscured by the monotony of echo; the incongruity between the form one expects a discussion to assume and the mechanical actuality of the non-dialogue may cause one to laugh. The Dindenault episode is terminated by the use of two other farcical ploys, brisk reversal and impudent last word. The deal succesfully closed and peace on the horizon, suddenly Panurge throws his aquisition into the ocean and all the other sheep, along with Dindenault himself, follow it to their deaths. Gleefully observing his victory, Panurge shouts the impudent last word:

> Panurge, à cousté du fougon, tenent un aviron en main . . . pour les enguarder de grimper sus la nauf et evader le naufraige, les preschoit eloquentement . . . leurs remonstrant par lieux de rhetoricque les miseres de ce monde, le bien et l'heur de l'autre vie, affermant plus heureux estre les trespassez que les vivans en ceste vallée de misere. (*Le Quart Livre*, 57)

If the reader is caught completely off-guard by Panurge's surprise trick, he may release the tension of emotional surprise (incongruous turn of events) through laughter. On the other hand, many readers will not laugh at this scene; Panurge has carried his practical jokes too far — he bears little resemblance to the roguish fun-lover of *Pantagruel.* One will possibly find it difficult to have feelings of superiority to or fantasies of aggression against Dindenault; his crime of vanity does not merit his punishment. The horror implicit in the content of this episode may well obscure the comic ploys of the form. How can one laugh with a man who explains as he murders his victim that after all this is done with the victim's well-being in mind?

Finally, two other aspects of farce mentioned by Stevenson characterize all Rabelais's work, extreme exaggerations and brutal directness. Characters are caricatures of normal physical appearance or behavior; language itself is caricatured in the harsh directness of obscenity and satirical attack.

While Stevenson's list of farcical ingredients tends to emphasize the importance of language in farce, other commentators stress the use of burlesque action. In chapter xix of *Pantagruel* Panurge debates with Thaumaste through the medium of physical gestures, making funny faces and funny noises:

> Dont Panurge mist les deux maistres doigtz à chascun cousté de la bouche, le retirant tant qu'il pouvoit en monstrant toutes ses dentz, et des deux poulses

rabaissoit les paulpiers des yeulx bien parfondement, en faisant assez layde grimace, selon que sembloit es assistans. (*Pantagruel,* 324)

Again, Panurge uses his fingers, this time to achieve the effect of a strange sound:

Adoncques Panurge mist le doigt indice de la dextre dedans la bouche, le serrant bien fort avecques les muscles de la bouche. Puis le tiroit, et, le tirant, faisoit un grand son, comme quand les petitz garsons tirent d'un canon de sulz avecques belles rabbes, et le fist par neuf foys. (*Pantagruel,* 323)

There are many sources of potential laughter in this episode. First, one laughs at the inappropriateness of two adults, conducting a supposedly serious, intellectual debate, who in actuality look like children or clowns at play. When Panurge turns the affair into a farce, one is not greatly surprised, but one may well be shocked when a famous scholar denigrates himself before the public: "Thaumaste, de grand hahan, se leva, mais en se levant fist un gros pet de boulangier, car le bran vint après, et pissa vinaigre bien fort, et puoit comme tous les diables" (*Pantagruel,* 322). Secondly, one laughs from the safety of his superiority to the scholar as well as from the tension created by the breaking of a public code of decency. Thirdly, one may laugh with Panurge as one might participate in the joy of a child who succeeds in turning a serious adult discussion into a "circus" by using playful antics and various attention getting devices. Thus, Rabelais uses Panurge's burlesque tactics to make the reader laugh at the expense of a scholar in search of absolute truth. Rabelais seems to suggest that one might better find a more natural concept of truth if he does not take himself too seriously.

Panurge is consistently involved in situations which draw much of their comic appeal from burlesque action, such as the tricks played on others in *Pantagruel.* His favorite tricks seem to involve duping hypocritical theologians, pretentious academicians or vain ladies. In chapter xvi:

En un aultre [bougette], il avoit tout plein de euphorbe pulverisé bien subtilement, et là dedans mettoit un mouschenez beau et bien ouvré . . . et, quand il se trouvoit en compaignie de quelques bonnes dames, il leur mettoit sus le propos de lingerie et leur mettoit la main au sein, demandant: "Et cest ouvraige, est il de Flandres, ou de Haynault?" Et puis tiroit son mouschenez, disant: "Tenez, tenez, voyez en cy de l'ouvrage; elle est de Foutignan ou de Foutarabie," et le secouoit bien fort à leurs nez, et les faisoit esternuer quatre heures sans repos.

Panurge compounds the humor in the situation, making himself, as well as the ladies, a target for laughter:

> Ce pendent il petoit comme un roussin, et les femmes ryoient luy disans: "Comment, vous petez, Panurge? "

Finally, one laughs at the incongruity of Panurge's unexpected reply; an elemental physical act is rationally explained:

> — "Non foys, disoit il, madame; mais je accorde au contrepoint de la musicque que vous sonnés du nez." (*Pantagruel*, 305-06)

In *Le Tiers Livre* Panurge himself is not the agent of burlesque action, for he has become victim rather than victor. No longer the fun-loving trickster of *Pantagruel*, he becomes a caricature of an adult, a pathetic figure. Doubting, ineffectual, ridiculously dressed in a bizarre attire of sackcloth and spectacles, this middle-aged man expressing the concerns and fears of a romantic youth may elicit laughter because of his exaggerated, incongruous condition or pity if one identifies with his fears. There is nonetheless burlesque action when Nazdecabre and Triboullet dispense a few blows along with their advice to Panurge. In chapter xx, Nazdecabre, deaf and dumb from birth, must speak through signs:

> La main ainsi composée posa sus le nombril de Panurge, mouvant continuelle-ment le poulce susdict, et appuyant icelle main sus les doigtz petit et indice, comme sus deux jambes. Ainsi montoit d'icelle main successivement à travers le ventre, le stomach, la poictrine, et le coul de Panurge .... En fin Panurge s'escria disant: "Par Dieu, maistre fol, vous serez battu, si ne me laissez." (*Le Tiers Livre*, 486)

In chapter xlv, Panurge consults Triboullet, a fool, who "luy bailla un grand coup de poing entre les deux espaules, luy rendit en main la bouteille, le nazardoit avecques la vessie de porc" (*Le Tiers Livre*, 588). This kind of purely physical farcical humor appeals to one's sense of the comic on a basic level: feelings and fantasies of an asocial nature are vicariously, albeit unconsciously, appeased. Secondly, one may laugh at these scenes because of the incongruity expressed. A fool who is supposed to be wise behaves like a fool; the wisdom of the "prophets" is revealed as sham. One's expectations are thwarted and the "realization" drains off in laughter.

In *Le Quart Livre* Panurge throws self-respect to the wind, revealing himself as a personification of burlesque ridiculousness. In chapter vi Dindenault insults Panurge by comparing him to his sheep who say "Bah, bah, bah". This seems like a prefiguration of the character he is to become later in *Le Quart Livre*, crying and sobbing, "Bebe be bous bous". When one sees Panurge huddled in a corner of the boat, babbling

and sobbing, one will probably be conscious of the disproportion between one's expectations from a grown man and the reality of Panurge's child-like cowardice; if one laughs, he expresses the aggressive defense of ridicule for the person who is "not me". One may also laugh in
the relief of denying his own fears of the unknown. Panurge's appearance at the end of *Le Quart Livre* will either incur outright laughter or
the reader will find so little to relate to in his ludicrous, demented state
that he would no more laugh at Panurge than at a person in a mental
hospital:

> Panurge, comme un boucq estourdy, sort de la soutte en chemise, ayant seule-
> ment un demy bas de chausses en jambe, sa barbe toute mouschetée de miettes
> de pain, tenent en main un grand chat soubelin, attaché à l'aultre demy bas de
> ses chausses. Et remuant les babines comme un cinge qui cherche poulz en teste,
> tremblant et clacquetant des dens, se tira vers frere Jan. (*Le Quart Livre,* 244)

It has been said that in laughter the ego experiences itself as all-suffi-
cient, as a total entity; likewise, a secure person or a child in control of
his surroundings feel complete. When security is threatened, when
childhood omnipotence is revealed as transitory, one becomes less complete, his image of self somewhat fragmented; one must then seek to
remold, reconstruct the shaken image of self. When Panurge expresses
the feeling of uncertainty, of seeking to find his emotional niche, he
loses much of his comic spirit. In *Le Tiers Livre* and *Le Quart Livre* he
is no longer the secure, omnipotent, farcical character portrayed in
Pantagruel. As he becomes unhappy, unsure, the pliable clown takes on
the rigidity of flesh and blood uncertainty and fear. Paradoxically,
when he temporarily loses the capacity to bounce back, he transcends
his "flatness" as a character and becomes almost real. Real characters
have feelings, real characters do not always bounce back. One might
even suggest that Panurge can be viewed as a semi-tragic figure.

Arthur Koestler speaks for many critics who include sympathy, i-
dentification, pity and admiration in those feelings elicited by tragedy.
He finds that the common denominator in those emotions imputed to
tragedy is a conscious feeling of participation, identification, belonging.
The tension involved in recognition of the tragic is resolved in the
catharsis of merging:

> In other words, the self is experienced as being a "part of a larger whole," a
> higher unity — which may be Nature, God, Mankind, Universal Order, or the
> "Anima Mundi"; it may be an abstract idea, or a human bond with persons
> living, dead or imagined. I propose to call the common element in these emo-
> tions the "participatory" or "self-transcending" tendencies. This is not meant in

a mystical sense . . . the term is merely intended to convey that in these emotional states the need is felt to behave "as a part" of some real or imaginary entity which transcends, as it were, the boundaries of the individual self;[40]

While there is collision of two habitually incompatible matrices in comedy, there is fusion in tragedy. Although emotions are usually a mixture of both self-transcending (tragic) emotions and self-assertive (comic) ones, those that predominate in a situation determine whether the viewer or reader will laugh, sigh or cry. For instance, the fat man slipping and crashing on the icy pavement will be either a comic or a tragic figure according to whether the spectator's attitude is dominated by malice (I'm glad that it's not I.) or pity (The poor man!). Koestler says: "A callous schoolboy will laugh at the spectacle, a sentimental old lady may be inclined to weep."[41] Citing a literary example, he says:

> Don Quixote gradually changes from a comic into a puzzling figure if, instead of relishing his delusions with arrogant condescension, I become interested in their psychological causes; and he changes into a tragic figure as detached curiosity turns into sympathetic identification – as I recognize in the sad knight my brother-in-arms in the fight against wind-mills.[42]

In aligning oneself with the tragic emotions, one can feel noble, or at least sympathetic, through conscious identification, whereas in comedy one denies association with the comic person or situation thereby fleeing himself, albeit through recognition.

As Panurge becomes less farcical, more complex, a reader's reaction to him will be more individual, more unique. As farcical character Panurge is usually funny. Even if one does not laugh at his sadistic tricks or his tall tales, the leveling factor of sexual indiscretion will probably make almost everyone laugh at some point. As frustrated figure in *Le Tiers Livre,* Panurge is not as amusing as he was in *Pantagruel.* Dressed in a strange attire, he does look ridiculous and one might laugh at the incongruity, the impersonation. However, as he becomes increasingly insecure and frightened (child-like), the reader might adapt toward him the attitude which Freud calls humor: the reader, secure in the fictional world and in his own emotional identity, can smile paternally at the painful crisis involved in seeking one's identity, aware that the situation is not after all tragic. On the other hand, if the reader is forging his own emotional image, is yet seeking and uncertain, he may

40. Koestler, p. 54.
41. Koestler, p. 46.
42. Koestler, p. 46.

identify with Panurge's frustration and fear and find him a somewhat tragic character. The reader may laugh with the Panurge of *Le Quart Livre* when he expresses feelings of joy. For example, when the storm is over and Panurge's confidence is restored, he is exuberant:

> Comment, vous ne faictez rien, frere Jan? Est il bien temps de boire à ceste heure? Que sçavons nous si l'estaffier de sainct Martin nous brasse encores quelque nouvelle oraige? Vous iray je encores ayder de là? Vertus guoy! je me repens bien, mais c'est à tard, que n'ay suivy la doctrine des bons philosophes, qui disent soy pourmener près la mer, et naviger près la terre estre chose moult sceure, et delectable, comme aller à pied quand l'on tient son cheval par la bride. Ha, ha, ha, par Dieu, tout va bien. Vous aideray je encores là? Baillez ça, je feray bien cela, ou le Diable y sera. (*Le Quart Livre,* 109)

Also, Panurge's excessive fear and infantile reactions are so ludicrous that the reader may laugh from embarrassed discomfort or from his position of superiority. However, much of Panurge's behavior in this book is so extreme and so irrational that the reader will possibly feel only sympathy or pity. In *Pantagruel* the reader could laugh at Panurge's ludicrous actions and asocial behavior because Panurge was a successful character — in control, assertive, forceful, thus real to the emotions as a victor in life's struggle. As he gradually becomes a caricature of himself, he loses the reality of such charm and also much of his comic impact. Whether or not the reader laughs at Panurge's often ludicrous state in *Le Quart Livre,* it is possible that the laughter will not be very forceful; when a mixture of emotions is aroused (disdain/pity, superiority/sympathy), the emotional impulse to laugh is diluted.

A conclusion to this chapter demands some consideration of the importance of character in comedy and ultimately the place of comic character in the text itself. Although much of what is funny in a fictional comedy is derived from the use of language in jokes, puns and nonsense statements, this application of language does not exist apart from characters in situations; at some point, the language, situation and character become synonymous. In other words, funny exchanges or situations do not exist without funny people to make them so. Sypher maintains that:

> If tragedy requires plot first of all, comedy is rooted so firmly in "character" its plot seems derivative, auxiliary, perhaps incidental. Unlike tragedy, comedy does not have to guard itself by any logic of inevitability, or by academic rules. Comedy makes artistic all the unlikely possibilities that tragic probability must reject. It keeps more of the primitive aspect of "play" than does tragedy.[43]

43. Sypher, "The Meanings of Comedy," pp. 219-20.

Bergson and Meredith dispensed with the comic figure by calling him a type, a puppet, a mechanical automaton, with little more relevance to the whole of a work than any other technical device of style. Yet more recent critics such as Koestler and Langer attribute to the comic hero some complexity of character. Panurge rises above the level of mere "flat" character or simple buffoon and becomes a comic hero partially because he embodies certain feelings and fantasies which are embedded in human nature. One has said that fantasies of aggression and rebellion are in some degree common to all. Also, most human beings have feelings of embarrassment or anger which are frequently repressed in the service of social propriety. When the asocial fantasies or repressed feelings of a reader are expressed by a literary character, the reader may unconsciously recognize himself in the character and in reaction may vicariously live out a fantasy or relieve a feeling of emotional tension by smiling or laughing. The greater the tension which is released through laughter, the louder the laugh and the more satisfying the momentary resolution. In the case of Panurge's aggression and sadism, one may laugh to deny his own fantasies and feelings; at the same time he may laugh as a token of participation in the rebellious jest. Whether one is laughing at Panurge's having put dung in the hoods of eminent theologians or at his having tricked the cardboard character of Dindenault into drowning, one is manifesting his own attitude toward unacceptable impulses and through the work of fiction is mastering these impulses by indirectly living them out, relaxed in his invincibility.

If Panurge were only an aggressive trickster, he would remain fixed, monolinear; however, he is also insecure, brave, ridiculous, charming, ultimately rigid in his child-likeness yet pliable by virtue of standing on a ledge where any change is possible. Consequently, he has interested readers throughout several centuries – a charming, yet inexplicable character, from one perspective an anti-hero, yet from another the comic hero of Rabelais's work. Panurge, as rogue and buffoon and as emotional child trying to be an adult, is well described by Sypher's characterization of a comic hero as one who has a double nature: tempter and clown, hero and knave, child and man. His complexity results from his double nature:

> When he appears as tempter, the fool – the comic hero who stands "outside" – must put on the mask. He disguises himself as clown or devil, wearing as need arises the garb of buffoon, ironist, madman .... In tempting us the Adversary [the comic hero] must have the features of innocence, must charm us with mannerly good will, gaiety, finesse and high spirits. He may seem as honest as

Iago whose motiveless malignity wears the bland mask of friendship . . . . This Adversary may speak folly or profanity, or jest insanely, as did Nietzsche, who tempted the whole respectable middle class with his madness . . . . The Adversary must be expelled. The tempter must perish. That is we must sacrifice him to save ourselves.[44]

Panurge is largely comic when he is farcical; the reader laughs in a rejection of the Panurge who is "not me" and simultaneously admits the reality of the fantasies and feelings which "are me". Through laughter the reader manifests his own double nature, admitting his folly and profanity while denying it; he punishes the devil in himself as he rewards his malice through recognition; he destroys his good social self as he creates for himself an escape hatch.

The comic hero, a clown, is busy in the extreme. Above all, says Koestler, a clown is "the man of gigantic efforts and diminutive accomplishments."[45] Panurge endeavors to play the funniest trick in the world, pull the cleverest robbery, cover the earth and beyond, seeking advice which is never put into action. When one examines the results of this tireless energy, one finds no creative productivity, no meaningful contribution. The Puritan ethic must condemn this comic hero as a worthless do-nothing; and the adult reader must register and reject any impulse toward dilettantism, toward shirking responsibility, toward eschewing decisions. At the same time, the clown is seductive. He must assure himself that he is not the outsider he knows he really is:

Deep within himself the clown feels . . . that he does not quite belong to the group, but to avoid being left out of things altogether, he develops certain aptitudes that he hopes will endear him to the others, or at least make him indispensable. He learns to sing songs, tell stories, make puns, and play foolish practical jokes. In other words he plays somewhat the part of the clown or fool at mediaeval feasts. He does not quite belong nor is he taken seriously, but he is the general favourite . . . . The clown shrinks from assuming intellectual leadership, yet since he must make his audience laugh at all costs, he falls back on the one device remaining at his disposal, namely, that of making himself ridiculous. He invokes laughter with his grimaces and capers and costumes, but the laughter is at his own expense. The entertainer has become a buffoon and the pathetic superiority for which he strives so laboriously costs him . . . his human dignity.[46]

44. Sypher, pp. 36-37.
45. Koestler, p. 81.
46. Fritz Künkel, *What it Means to Grow Up: A Guide to Understanding the Development of Character*, trans., Barbara Keppel-Compton and Hulda Niebuhr (New York: Charles Scribner's Sons, 1944), pp. 88-89.

The clown, like the child, seeks attention to prove his worth to himself. One has said that insofar as Panurge is child-like, the reader relates to him through a residue of feelings and fantasies in himself that might be labeled child-like. The comic situation itself is one which returns an adult to his childhood, for much that is comic is based on embarrassed discomfort, a situation in which one feels again the helplessness of the child. The worst of these embarrassments is the disturbance of adult activities through the imperative demands of natural wants. For example, Panurge passes gas in public and onlookers as well as readers may titter in discomfort. There is also the laughter of joy and pleasure which is paralleled in childhood activity. For instance, where the comic situation acts through repetitions, it is based on the pleasure of constant repetition peculiar to the child (asking questions, telling stories, compulsively reiterating certain phrases in games).[47] According to Freud, the comedy of exaggeration also has its roots in childhood fantasy:

> Exaggeration, which also affords pleasure even to the grown-up in so far as it is justified by his reason, corresponds to the characteristic want of moderation in the child, and its ignorance of all quantitative relations which it later really learns to know as qualitative. To keep within bounds, to practice moderation even in permissible feelings is a late fruit of education, and is gained through opposing inhibitions of the psychic activity acquired in the same association.[48]

As one reads about giants and superhuman capers, he may smile or laugh having become once more the child in a world of adult giants, or the child in a world of fantasy. Commenting on Freud's theory that the pleasure involved in laughter is in some way derived from a resurrection of a childish or infantile state of mind, Piddington says that since childhood is essentially a carefree period, it is not difficult to understand that a sudden revival of the carefree state of childhood should produce pleasure manifested in laughter.[49]

Yet Panurge is not always funny in *Le Tiers Livre* and only occasionally in *Le Quart Livre*. As charming trickster and gay rebel in *Pantagruel,* he is the "natural" child, spontaneous, clever and funny. In *Le Tiers Livre* his childlikeness is not so engaging, for it belongs to the realm of annoying, endless questions. One laughs at the Panurge of *Pantagruel*, thus nurturing his sense of security and acceptance as well as his fantasy of omnipotence. When he becomes stubborn, repetitive,

47. Freud, "Wit and its Relation to the Unconscious," p. 796.
48. Freud, "Wit and its Relation to the Unconscious," p. 796.
49. Piddington, p. 41.

whining, in *Le Tiers Livre,* one may lose interest in Panurge or may simply transfer his attention to other matters. In *Le Quart Livre* Panurge, the clown, the child, must woo his companions and the reader back into his sphere. If he acts like an adult, then he becomes like his companions, like the reader, and by definition not unique. If he jokes and plays tricks as in *Pantagruel,* he may regain the reader's attention, but he is too alienated from his position of well-being to do this. His only recourse seems to lie in becoming so ludicrous that one cannot but notice him, whether or not one laughs. To see a resemblance between the infantile Panurge of *Le Quart Livre* and the comic hero of *Pantagruel,* one must consider him in terms of the whole work.

Panurge as rogue, child or clown is a comic hero in the sense that he has a vitality lacking to the tragic hero. Harvey expresses the opinion that, "We really, I believe, admire the comic characters more than we do the [tragic] hero or heroine, because of their obstinate power to do-it-again, combined with a total lack of self-consciousness or shame."[50] Whether Panurge is sadistic trickster, inappropriate child or infantile coward, he personifies emotional feeling, body consciousness of being alive. In its ideal form the comic spirit might be described as an awareness of vitality, of triumphing over obstacles, of surviving. Susanne Langer describes laughter as the personification of emotional feeling:

> Laughter is not a simple overt act, as the single word suggests; it is the spectacular end of a complex process. As speech is the culmination of a mental activity, laughter is a culmination of feeling — the crest of a wave of felt vitality. A sudden sense of superiority entails such a "lift" of vital feeling. But the "lift" may occur without self-flattery too . . . . The baby laughs because his wish is gratified . . . . Sudden pleasure raises his general feeling tone, so he laughs.[51]

When one laughs, Miss Langer continues, one is living at the level of natural man, subjugated by no social or moral rules. And if man triumphs over his own weakness or his neighbor's ridiculousness in laughter, it is only a symbolic triumph of the larger victory which affirms in the face of destiny and fortune the will to survive.[52] Panurge, as comic hero, is resilient and innovative. He teaches that one must learn to bounce back, to survive, be he Picrochole or Pantagruel. Picrochole is defeated by his own rigidity; Pantagruel becomes dull with learned

---

50. W. J. Harvey, *Character and the Novel* (London: Chatto and Windus, 1965), pp. 59-60.
51. Langer, p. 340.
52. Langer, pp. 348-49.

maxims. Both rigidity and stuffiness are counter to the life rhythm of gaiety and spontaneity, of suffering hurts and disappointments only to try again. Thus, Panurge seems to be the emotional counterpart of Diogenes, rolling his tub furiously, going nowhere but always ready to go anywhere. The indomitable rogue, roasted by the Turks, frightened by the vastness of the unknown, bounces back again and again. At the end of *Le Quart Livre* his quest is far from completed, but there is no real tragedy in this; one knows that come what may, his emotionally pure zest for life will make of him a survivor.

Finally, Panurge is a comic hero because an assertion of the will to survive demands not only that one accept vicissitudes, but also that one accept contradictions. Sypher observes: "The comic hero and the saint accept the irreconcilables in man's existence . . . . Comic artist and religious hero look at man's struggle from infinite distance and revise its human weight or its penalties."[53] Thus, in terms of Rabelais's whole work, Panurge can be viewed as portraying an emotional lesson which is parallel to Rabelais's intellectual message: there is no absolute "truth", only relativity and the obvious necessity for accepting paradox and contradiction. Rabelais's resolution to philosophical paradox is the synthesis of comedy. But, one must ask, does comedy offer any real resolution to the human struggle? Does it protect society's values or level them? Is Rabelais conservative or revolutionary? The answer to these questions must once more be a paradox as is the work; comedy protects and levels, Rabelais is conservative and revolutionary. Laughter maintains the *status quo* by denying unconscious disturbances, by correcting one's just shaken view of self and world. By laughing one adopts an attitude which from infancy has expressed the feeling of satisfaction with things as they are. Physiologically laughter induces a condition of euphoria, which reinforces the belief that everything is as it should be; thus, society preserves the good manners, morals, conceptions of rank and so on, of its members.[54] At the same time the physiological process of laughter serves each individual by providing him with a socially acceptable manner in which to release the tensions of embarassment, hostility, aggression and joy.

When one's laughter is levelled at a fictional character, one feels not so much freedom from danger of whatever may break through his carefully constructed social facade, as security in the face of danger.

53. Sypher, "The Meanings of Comedy," pp. 237 and 239.
54. Piddington, pp. 129-30.

Panurge may call into question some cherished values of self and society, but after all what does one really have to fear from someone who carries a flask and a piece of ham under his cloak and calls them his bodyguard? Panurge is Rabelais's will to conquer and his concomitant failure to conquer; he represents the sacrifice and feast of the fertility rites from which comedy and tragedy are said to have been born, the cycle of death and rebirth. At the end of *Le Quart Livre* Panurge is alive, is ready to continue his quest. Comedy is redemption, a triumph over mortality. And thus comic art is the spirit of art itself – the insistence on eternity, on permanence.

Possibly Rabelais is a great comic author because he so thoroughly embodies the comic spirit in the whole of his work – that recognition of one's rebelliousness and one's joy. The comic spirit ultimately becomes a permit to the uniqueness of one's feelings and fantasies. At the same time, Rabelais exposes the common base behind individual feelings and fantasies. In the privacy of one's subjective world, one may laugh at the practical jokes and sexual boasts of Panurge; however, when one remembers that others have laughed at the same things in various ages and societies, one must agree that comedy strips off the war-paint and the feathers, the college degrees or the military medals and shows how very like at bottom the hero is to everybody else.[55] At the end of *Le Quart Livre* Panurge loses complete control of his emotions and of his bowels, appearing as an infant or a madman. There is so little with which to identify that the reader may not even be tempted to laugh at his ludicrous state. However, true to his comic nature, reaffirming his emotional zest, Panurge refuses to be conquered and in the last words of *Le Quart Livre* he reasserts his egotism, his rebellion against tradition (society would give dirty names to my excrement while I call it saffron.) and his joy:

> – Dictez vous, respondit Panurge, que j'ay paour? Pas maille. Je suys, par la vertus Dieu, plus couraigeux que si j'eusse autant de mousches avallé qu'il en est mis en paste dedans Paris, depuys la feste S. Jan jusques à la Toussains. Ha, ha, ha! Houay! Que diable est cecy? Appelez vous cecy foyre, bren, crottes, merde, fiant, dejection, matiere fecale, excrement, repaire, laisse, esmeut, fumée, estron, scybale ou spyrathe? C'est, croy je, sapphran d'Hibernie. Ho, ho, hie! C'est sapphran d'Hibernie! Sela! Beuvons. (*Le Quart Livre*, 248)

And one laughs with Panurge, attesting to the incorrigible element in man, affirming the will to survive.

---

55. Enck, p. 116.

CONCLUSION

The problem of critical attitude in regard to Rabelais transcends individual bias insofar as the question of mode of interpretation is one of the central themes of Rabelais's work. My study has attempted to add to the vast body of Rabelaisian scholarship the idea that Rabelais's genius stands the test of time not only because of its intellectual and stylistic richness and diversity, but also because there is an underlying emotional unity that binds the various books and which is communicated to the reader through the interplay of the various characters and particularly through Panurge.[1]

In concluding this study it may once again be useful to look to psychological theory to clarify further the meaning of Panurge in Rabelais's total work and to supply additional proof for the idea that there can be a commonality of emotional childhood and adolescent experience between a sixteenth century character and a twentieth century reader. If one considers the psychological influence of social situation, the unrest of the Renaissance period can easily be viewed as having psychological parallels with the turmoil so typical of twentieth century socieites. Seeking, doubting, fearing, rebelling, yet always bouncing back, the spirit of the Renaissance is symbolized by Rabelais's frenzied pen and brought to life visually by Panurge.

Kenneth Keniston looks to psychological response which is linked more directly to human development than to specific social circumstance. In an article entitled "Youth: A 'New' Stage of Life," Keniston discusses the phenomena of adolescence, the fluid period between childhood and adulthood. He notes that before 1904 there was no specific term to describe this stage of development, although no one

---

1. Diana Spearman expresses the opinion that: "Few critics today believe in Hegel's Absolute but do believe that all social and cultural phenomena, even though they appear to spring from different sources and serve different ends, are inspired by a common psychological ethos or outlook." Diana Spearman, *The Novel and Society* (New York: Barnes & Noble, Inc., 1966), p. 5.

today doubts its existence.[2] Keniston suggests that one may view adolescence in a positive sense, looking beyond the traditional, negative emphasis on rebellion and turmoil. He even suggests a new term for the stage between destructive childhood or adolescence and adulthood — the term is "youth".[3] The significance of Keniston's concept of "youth" is that he describes a stage which is not defined by role, class, position or age, but is rather a psychological orientation.[4] He then gives historical examples which are meant to prove that the stage of adolescence has always existed and that implicitly so has the psychological disposition which he calls "youth". However, says Keniston, the specific concerns of "youth" will be delineated by its society and by its historical era.[5] The important thing about the spirit of "youth" is that its doubts lead to questioning which often results in a positive kind of rebellion — a rebellion which can lead to intellectual and emotional growth and understanding. Thus, Keniston's concept of "youth" may serve as an appropriate description of Panurge's combined emotional and intellectual significance. Although Panurge does not indicate an awareness of "self" or of internal conflict, he does represent the dilemma of being in conflict with one's society.

In opposition to the openness which "youth" represents, Keniston says that adulthood is traditionally defined as a psychological stage reached when one finds answers to questions — questions of relationship to the existing society, questions of vocation, social role and life style.[6] While Panurge as agent of the comic and as rogue is expressive of the rebellious Renaissance spirit, he also portrays the Renaissance mood of openness and wonder (the spirit of "youth") and thus is said to express

---

2. Kenneth Keniston, "Youth: A 'New' Stage of Life," pp. 631-54 in *The American Scholar,* ed., Hiram Haydn, XXXIX (Autumn, 1970), 632.

3. Keniston, p. 635.

4. Keniston, p. 648.

5. Keniston says that a mark of "youth" is its attempt to break out of prescribed roles, out of culture, out of history: "Youth is a time, then, when earlier socialization and acculturation is self-critically analyzed, and massive efforts made to uproot the now alien traces of historicity, social membership and culture. Needless to say, these efforts are invariably accomplished within a social, cultural and historical context, using historically available methods. Youth's relationship to history is therefore paradoxical. Although it may try to reject history altogether, youth does so in a way defined by its historical era, and those rejections may even come to define that era." Keniston, p. 638.

6. Keniston, p. 634.

the positive emotional spirit of searching. It is he who comes on the scene unknown, alone, free; it is he who serves as pretext for an investigation of various traditional ideas and myths; it is he who is willing to continue his quest into uncharted territory. In *Pantagruel* Panurge speaks fourteen languages and tells tales of marvelous voyages and adventures. Recitals of conquests and of fantastic achievements outline for the reader a portrait of a character who has few limits in thought or deed. In *Le Tiers Livre* Panurge experiences ambivalent feelings about his own identity and his role in society. He feels alternately powerful and powerless, free and fettered. Ultimately, he refuses to accept society's idea of adulthood. Thus, he depicts Keniston's idea of "youth". And, to the degree that a reader questions, doubts, fluctuates and searches, he can respond intellectually *and* emotionally, through feeling and fantasy to the mood of "youth" expressed by Panurge.

While Panurge may be viewed as symbolic of the "Que sais-je? " attitude, Pantagruel functions as spokesman for the author who recognizes the lesson to be learned from Panurge; having created Pantagruel as representative of "new" truth, yet not wholly satisfied with this, Rabelais appropriately gave him as companion, Panurge. Panurge, moving and changing, yet unified in the emotional rhythm of his quest, teaches Pantagruel and the reader that movement, change, questioning and seeking are positive values in themselves. Panurge's illusion of liberty is the ultimate mark of the work, the only place where Rabelais finds the freedom to march forward, all the while aware that linear progress is in reality the closed circle of fantasy and fiction.

BIBLIOGRAPHY

Allport, Gordon W., et al. *Theories of Personality*. New York: John Wiley & Sons, Inc., 1957.

Arendt, Hannah. *The Human Condition: A Study of the Central Dilemmas Facing Modern Man*. Garden City, New York: Anchor Books, Doubleday and Company, Inc., 1959.

Auerbach, Eric. *Dante Poet of the Secular World*. Trans. Ralph Manheim. Chicago: The University of Chicago Press, 1961.

——— "The World in Pantagruel's Mouth." *Mimesis: The Representation of Reality in Western Literature*. Trans. Willard Trask. Garden City, New York: Anchor Books, Doubleday and Company, Inc., 1957, pp. 229-49.

Axline, Virginia M. *Play Therapy*. New York: Ballantine Books, Inc., 1969.

Ayau, A. E. *The Social Psychology of Hunger and Sex*. Cambridge, Mass.: Sci-Art Publishers, Printed by Independent Press, Boston, 1939.

Barthes, Rolland. *Essais critiques*. Paris: Editions du Seuil, 1964.

Beaujour, Michel. *Le Jeu de Rabelais*. Issoudun: Editions de l'Herne, 1969.

Bentley, Eric. "The Psychology of Farce." *The Genius of the French Theatre*. Ed. and Intro. Albert Bermel. New York: The New American Library of World Literature, Inc., 1961, pp. 540-53.

Benveniste, E. *Problèmes de linguistique générale*. Paris: Gallimard, 1966.

Bergson, Henri. *Le Rire: Essai sur la signification du comique*. Paris: Librairie Felix Alcan, 1932.

Besant, Walter. *Rabelais*. London: William Blackwood and Sons, 1879.

Booth, Wayne C. *The Rhetoric of Fiction*. Chicago: The University of Chicago Press, 1961.

Bowen, Elizabeth. "Notes on Writing a Novel." *Perspectives on Fiction*. Eds. James L. Calderwood and Harold E. Tolliver. New York: Oxford University Press, 1968, pp. 217-30.

Brown, J. A. C. *Freud and the Post-Freudians*. Baltimore: Penguin Books, 1967.

Brown, Norman Oliver. *Life Against Death: The Psychoanalytical Meaning of History*. New York: Random House, Inc., 1959.

——— *Love's Body*. New York: Random House, Inc., 1968.

Bury, J. B. *A History of Freedom of Thought*. New York: Henry Holt and Company, 1913.

Campbell, Joseph. "Man and Myth." *Psychology Today*, 5, 2 (July, 1971), 35-39 and 86-95.

Cary, Joyce. *Art and Reality: Ways of the Creative Process*. Garden City, New York: Anchor Books, Doubleday and Company, Inc., 1961.

Clement, Nemours H. "The Influence of the Arthurian Romances on the Five Books of Rabelais." *University of California Publications in Modern Philology*. Eds. William H. Durham, et al. 12, 3 (May 8, 1926), 147-257.

Crews, Frederick C. "Anaesthetic Criticism: I." *The New York Review of Books,* 14, 4 (Feb. 26, 1970), 31-35.

——— "Anaesthetic Criticism: II." *The New York Review of Books,* 14, 5 (March 12, 1970), 49-52.

——— "Literature and Psychology." *Relations of Literary Study: Essays on Interdisciplinary Contributions.* Ed. James Thorpe. New York: Modern Language Association, 1967, pp. 73-87.

Dieguez, Manuel de. *Rabelais par lui-même.* Paris: Editions du Seuil, 1960.

Doubrovsky, Serge. *Pourquoi la nouvelle critique: Critique et objectivité.* Paris: Mercure de France, 1967.

Edel, Leon. *The Psychological Novel: 1900-1950.* New York: J. B. Lippincott Company, 1967.

Enck, John J., et al, (Eds.). *The Comic in Theory and Practice.* New York: Appleton-Century-Crofts, Inc., 1960.

Erikson, Erik H. *Childhood and Society.* New York: W. W. Norton and Company, Inc., 1963.

Fenichel, Otto. *The Psychoanalytic Theory of Neurosis.* New York: W. W. Norton and Company, Inc., 1945.

Fiedler, Leslie A. *No! in Thunder.* Boston: Beacon Press, 1960.

Fleury, Jean. *Rabelais et ses oeuvres.* Paris: Didier et Cie, Librairies-Editeurs, 1877.

Forster, E. M. *Aspects of the Novel.* New York: Harcourt, Brace and Company, 1927.

Freud, Sigmund. *Dora: An Analysis of a Case of Hysteria.* New York: Collier Books, 1966.

——— *Early Psychoanalytical Writings.* Ed. and Intro. Edward P. Rieff. New York: Collier Books, 1963.

——— "Humour." *Collected Papers.* The International Psycho-Analytical Library. Ed. James Strachey. Toronto: Clarke, Irwin and Company, Ltd., 1950, V, 215-21.

——— "Wit and its Relation to the Unconscious." *The Basic Writings of Sigmund Freud.* Ed. and Trans. A. A. Brill. New York: The Modern Library, Random House, Inc., 1938, pp. 633-803.

Frohock, W. M. "Panurge as Comic Character." *Yale French Studies,* 23 (1959), 71-76.

Fromm, Erich. *The Revolution of Hope: Toward a Humanized Technology.* New York: Harper and Row, 1968.

Frye, Northrop. *The Well-Tempered Critic.* Bloomington, Indiana: Indiana University Press, 1963.

Funk & Wagnalls Standard College Dictionary. Eds. Shelia C. Brantley, et al. Chicago: Harcourt, Brace and World, Inc., 1968.

Glauser, Alfred. *Rabelais créateur.* Paris: Editions A.-G. Nizet, 1966.

Gray, Floyd. *Rabelais et l'Ecriture.* Paris: Librairie A.-G. Nizet, 1974.

Hall, Calvin S. *A Primer of Freudian Psychology.* New York: A Mentor Book, The New American Library of World Literature, Inc., 1959.

Harvey, W. J. *Character and the Novel.* London: Chatto and Windus, 1965.

Haydn, Hiram. *The Counter-Renaissance.* New York: Harcourt, Brace and World, Inc., 1950.

Heilman, Robert B. "Felix Krull: Variations on Picaresque." *Perspectives on Fiction*. Eds. James L. Calderwood and Harold E. Tolliver. New York: Oxford University Press, 1968, pp. 101-09.

Henry, Jules. "The Term 'Primitive' in Kierkegaard and Heidegger." *The Concept of Primitive*. Ed. Ashley Montagu. New York: The Free Press, 1968, pp. 212-28.

Holland, Norman N. *The Dynamics of Literary Response*. New York: Oxford University Press, 1968.

––– "Unity Identity Text Self." PMLA, 90 (1975), 813-22.

Huizinga, Johan. *Homo Ludens: A Study of the Play-Element in Culture*. Boston: The Beacon Press, 1950.

Janeway, Elizabeth. "Happiness and the Right to Choose." *Atlantic Monthly*, March, 1970, pp. 118-26.

Josipovici, G. D. "Rabelais." *French Literature and its Background: 1 The Sixteenth Century*. Ed. John Cruickshank. New York: Oxford University Press, 1968.

Jung, Carl G. and C. Kerényi. *Essays on a Science of Mythology: The Myths of the Divine Child and the Divine Maiden*. Trans. R. F. C. Hull. New York: Harper and Row, 1949.

Koestler, Arthur. *The Act of Creation*. New York: Dell Publishing Company, Inc., 1967.

Keniston, Kenneth. "Youth: A 'New' Stage of Life." *The American Scholar*. Ed. Hiram Haydn. 39 (Autumn, 1970), 631-54.

Künkel, Fritz. *What it Means to Grow Up: A Guide to Understanding the Development of Character*. Trans. Barbara Keppel-Compton and Hulda Niebuhr. New York: Charles Scribner's Sons, 1944.

Lagarde, André and Laurent Michard. *Moyen Age: Les Grands Auteurs français du programme*. Bordas: Collection Textes et Littérature, 1962.

Laing, R. D. *The Divided Self: An Existential Study in Sanity and Madness*. Baltimore: Penguin Books, 1970.

Langer, Susanne K. *Feeling and Form: A Theory of Art*. New York: Charles Scribner's Sons, 1953.

L'Association des Amis de Rabelais et de la Devinière. *Les Amis de Rabelais et de la Devinière*. Bulletin No. 3, II (1964).

Lebègue, Raymond. *Rabelais*. Tübingen: Max Niemeyer Verlag, 1952.

Lefranc, Abel. *Rabelais: Etudes sur Gargantua, Pantagruel, Le Tiers Livre*. Paris: A Michel, 1953.

Lenoir, Paulette. *Quelques Aspects de la pensée de Rabelais*. Paris: Editions Sociales, 1954.

Lesser, Simon O. *Fiction and the Unconscious*. New York: Random House, Inc., 1962.

Malloch, A. E. "The Techniques and Function of the Renaissance Paradox." *Studies in Philology*. Ed. Dougald MacMillan. Chapel Hill: The University of North Carolina Press, 1956. LIII,191-203.

Manheim, Leonard. "Psychoanalytic Criticism Comes of Age." *Psychiatry and Social Science Review*. 2, 11 (Nov., 1968) 9-11.

Marcuse, Herbert. *Eros and Civilization: A Philosophical Inquiry into Freud*. Boston: The Beacon Press, 1955.

Mauron, Charles. *Des Métaphores obsédantes au mythe personnel: Introduction à la Psychocritique.* Paris: Librairie José Corti, 1963.

May, Rollo. *Love and Will.* New York: W. W. Norton and Company, Inc., 1969.

——— *Man's Search for Himself.* New York: The New American Library, Inc., 1967.

Mayrargues, Alfred. *Rabelais: Etude sur le seizième siècle.* Paris: Librairie Hachette et Cie, 1868.

Meredith, George. "An Essay on Comedy." *Comèdy.* Intro. and Appendix Wylie Sypher. Garden City, New York: Anchor Books, Doubleday and Company, Inc., 1956, pp. 3-57.

Montagu, Ashley. "The Fallacy of the 'Primitive'." *The Concept of the Primitive.* Ed. Ashley Montagu. New York: The Free Press, 1968, pp. 1-6.

Morton, G. F. *Childhood's Fears: Psycho-Analysis and the Inferiority-Fear Complex.* New York: Macmillan Company, 1925.

Muir, Edwin. *Essays on Literature and Society.* Cambridge, Mass.: Harvard University Press, 1965.

Paris, Jean. *Hamlet et Panurge.* Paris: Editions du Seuil, 1971.

Piaget, Jean. *La Formation du symbole chez l'enfant.* Neuchatel: Delachaus and Niestlé, S. N., 1945.

Piddington, Ralph. *The Psychology of Laughter: A Study in Social Adaptation.* New York: Gamut Press, Inc., 1963.

Plank, Robert. *The Emotional Significance of Imaginary Beings: A Study of the Interaction Between Psychopathology, Literature and Reality in the Modern World.* Springfield, Ill.: Charles C. Thomas, 1968.

Plattard, Jean. *François Rabelais.* Paris: Boivin & Cie, 1932.

Quincey, Thomas de. "Littérature de connaissance et littérature de puissance." *La Délirante: Revue de Poésie,* 3 (oct.-déc., 1968), 76-83.

Rabelais, François. *Gargantua, Oeuvres complètes.* vol. I of 2 vols. Ed. Pierre Jourda. Paris: Editions Garnier Frères, 1962.

——— *Le Cinquième Livre, Oeuvres complètes.* vol. II of 2 vols. Ed. Pierre Jourda. Paris: Editions Garnier Frères, 1962.

——— *Le Quart Livre, Oeuvres complètes.* vol. II of 2 vols. Ed. Pierre Jourda. Paris: Editions Garnier Frères, 1962.

——— *Le Tiers Livre, Oeuvres complètes.* vol. I of 2 vols. Ed. Pierre Jourda. Paris: Editions Garnier Frères, 1962.

——— *Pantagruel, Oeuvres complètes.* vol. I of 2 vols. Ed. Pierre Jourda. Paris: Editions Garnier Frères, 1962.

Rocques, Mario. "Aspects de Panurge." *Ouvrage publié pour le quatrième centenaire de sa mort, 1553-1953.* Genève: Librairie E. Droz, 1953.

Rosenberg, B. G. "Psychology Through the Looking Glass." *Psychology Today,* 5, 1 (June, 1971), 55-56 and 68.

Rychlak, Joseph F. *A Philosophy of Science for Personality Theory.* Boston: Houghton, Mifflin Company, 1968.

Saurraute, Nathalie. *L'Ere du soupçon: Essais sur le roman.* Paris: Gallimard. 1956.

Saulnier, Verdun L. *Le Dessein de Rabelais.* Paris: Société d'Editions d'Enseignement Supérieur, 1957.

Schrader, Ludwig. *Panurge und Hermes: Zum Ursprung eines Charakters bei Rabelais.* Bonn: Romanisches Seminar der Universität Bonn, 1958.

Screech, M. A. "Preparing a New Edition of Gargantua." Speech given at a Rabelais Symposium, November 6-8, 1969. State University of New York at Albany, New York. Dr. Screech spoke on November 6, 1969. After his speech, he discussed his ideas on various scholarly problems in Rabelais, one of which was Panurge.

––– *The Rabelaisian Marriage: Aspects of Rabelais's Religion, Ethics and Comic Philosophy.* London: Edward Arnold, Ltd., 1958.

Slater, Philip. *The Pursuit of Loneliness: American Culture at the Breaking Point.* Boston: Beacon Press, 1970.

Smith, William Francis. *Rabelais in His Writings.* New York: G. P. Putnam's sons, 1918.

Sontag, Susan. "Against Interpretation." *Against Interpretation and Other Essays.* New York: Dell Publishing Company, Inc., 1969, pp. 13-23.

Spearman, Diana. *The Novel and Society.* New York: Barnes and Noble, Inc., 1966.

Spitzer, Leo. "Le Prétendu Réalisme de Rabelais." *Modern Philology.* Chicago: The University of Chicago Press, 1940. IIIVII, 139-50.

Stapfer, Paul. *Rabelais: sa personne, son génie, son oeuvre.* Paris: Librairie Armand Colin, 1906.

Stevenson, Robert C. "Farce as Method." *The Tulane Drama Review.* Ed. Robert W. Corrigan. 5, 2 (Dec., 1960), 85-93.

Sypher, Wylie. "The Meanings of Comedy." *Comedy.* Intro. and Appendix Wylie Sypher. Garden City, New York: Anchor Books, Doubleday and Company, Inc., 1956, pp. 193-255.

Tetel, Marcel. *Rabelais.* New York: Twayne Publications, Inc., 1967.

The Random House Dictionary of the English Language: College Edition. Ed. Laurence Urdang. New York: Random House, Inc., 1968.

Trilling, Lionel. "Freud and Literature." *The Liberal Imagination: Essays on Literature and Society.* Garden City, New York: Anchor Books, Doubleday and Company, Inc., 1953. pp. 32-54.

Vexliard, Alexandre. *Le Clochard: Etude de psychologie sociale.* Paris: Desclée de Brouwer, 1957.

Watts, Alan. *The Book: On the Taboo Against Knowing Who You Are.* New York: Pantheon Books, 1966.

Webster's New World Dictionary of the American Language. New York: The World Publishing Company, 1960.

Wellek, René and Austin Warren. *Theory of Literature.* New York: Harcourt, Brace and World, Inc., 3rd ed., 1962.

Whitehead, Alfred North. *Science and the Modern World.* New York: A Mentor Book, The New American Library, 1967.